The Iliad
Interpreted for Entrepreneurs

Why Founder Pride and Internal Rivalries Destroy Businesses

ANCIENT WISDOM HACKS

Third Edition

Table of Contents

Preface – Why Bronze-Age War Poetry Still Matters to Startups

"Sing, O goddess, the anger of Achilles…"—the first line of *The Iliad* is a startup mission statement in miniature. It names the core conflict (anger), the chief protagonist (Achilles), and calls for divine energy (creativity) to drive the narrative forward. The poem is not a museum piece; it is a field manual for navigating high-stakes, high-ego ventures in volatile environments.

Startups, like the Achaean coalition on the beaches of Troy, run on limited time, scarce resources, and the unpredictable chemistry of big personalities. Homer shows what happens when vision outpaces logistics, when pride outruns purpose, and when a single decisive act—"Achilles … refused the gifts and swore a mighty oath" —can stall an entire campaign. By translating this drama into modern practice, we reclaim ancient pattern recognition: how to rally a fragmented team, outmaneuver incumbents, and turn personal drive into collective momentum.

How to Use This Book – Skim-Then-Apply Structure, Reflection Prompts, Sprint Templates

This playbook is built for founders who sprint, not stroll. Each chapter follows a consistent rhythm:

1. **The Scene** – A brief retelling of a key episode. Feel free to skim; it's there for narrative context.

2. **The Strategic Lesson** – One line you can underline and carry into the next stand-up meeting.

3. **Reflection Prompts** – Three questions that force you to map the epic onto your own venture. Example: after the embassy to Achilles, ask, "Where am I mistaking perks for purpose?"

4. **Sprint Template** – A concrete, two-week exercise. Cut-and-paste it into your project board, assign owners, set demo day.

Read sequentially or dart around. If your biggest pain today is churn, jump to Hector's defensive tactics. If you're prepping Series B, study Agamemnon's coalition management. The only rule: finish every reading session by scheduling an action. Without action, you're just another bard reciting glorious possibilities.

Key Characters & Business Parallels – A Quick Guide for Founder Archetypes

- **Achilles — Visionary Talent**
  "My mother tells me two fates shadow me…" Achilles holds the power of outsized impact, yet he knows the cost. Founders with super-skill must learn when to fight, when to

rest, and how to keep ego from freezing the whole camp.

- **Agamemnon — CEO**
  "I am king of men!" He commands resources but struggles with morale. His lesson: authority without empathy breeds mutiny. Measure your KPIs, but measure trust first.

- **Odysseus — COO**
  "Soft words are best for winning stubborn wills." The master of logistics, persuasion, and contingency planning. When the roadmap goes off-track, channel Odysseus: adapt, negotiate, improvise.

- **Nestor — Advisor**
  "I have seen better men than you, and they listened." Nestor's currency is long memory. Advisors convert experience into pattern detection, steering founders away from vanity metrics and toward durable fundamentals.

- **Hector — Market Incumbent**
  "I stand as defense for Troy and its honorable fathers." Hector embodies the dominant player—well-resourced, respected, and risk-averse. Study his strengths to spot your breakthrough angle; study his blind spots to ensure you never become him.

Use this cast list as a mirror. On any given day you may be Achilles forging ahead, Odysseus patching holes, or Agamemnon juggling investors. Keep the roles fluid, the mission fixed, and the story—your story—will stay worthy of song.

Chapter 1. "The Wrath of Achilles" — Define a Cause Worth Fighting For

The Opening Quarrel: Pride vs. Purpose

"Rage— goddess, sing the rage of Peleus' son Achilles…" The very first breath of *The Iliad* announces what is at stake: not the clash of armies, not the glitter of bronze, but an emotion so potent it can choke kings and topple empires. Achilles' wrath erupts when Agamemnon, "lord of men," strips him of Briseïs, the war-prize who has become both companion and symbol of honor.

"I for my part did not come here for the sake of the Trojan spearmen," Achilles spits. "I have no quarrel with them." He reminds Agamemnon—and himself—that he sailed to Troy for honor and glory, not plunder. Yet in the critical moment his personal pride overrides the shared purpose. He withdraws from battle, the Achaean front buckles, and the entire campaign teeters because one man's ego eclipses the collective mission.

Startup teams feel the same gravitational pull of ego. A gifted engineer storms out because product-marketing rewrites copy without asking. A co-founder refuses dilution even though fresh capital could extend runway. Investors circle like gods on Olympus, whispering flattery and fueling private ambitions. When pride eclipses purpose, momentum stalls, morale decays, and the market—the Trojan battlements—surges forward.

Homer refuses to glamorize this pride. He shows Achilles brooding by his ships, "gnawing at his heart," while comrades die. He shows Agamemnon swaggering, then despairing as he realizes his authority means nothing without the buy-in of talent. "I was mad, I myself will not deny it," the king admits when losses mount. In that confession lies the startup lesson: unchecked ego is expensive, and the invoice comes due in the darkest quarter.

Purpose, by contrast, pulls a fractured coalition back toward shared intent. When Achilles finally returns to battle, it is because the death of Patroclus rekindles a deeper why. "If heaven would grant me but to return home, my glory gone, yet vengeance shall be mine." The motive has shifted from personal slight to existential cause: to defend the living and honor the dead. The Greeks rally, ships burn no longer, and the tide of war turns because individual fury realigns with collective stakes.

Entrepreneurs rarely fight over captives or cattle, but they duel over roadmaps, titles, equity, and press. Every conflict forces a choice: pride or purpose. Pride seeks immediate vindication ("Ship it my way or I walk"). Purpose asks, "What advances the mission?" Pride makes the stand-up meeting a stage for one-upmanship. Purpose turns the same meeting into a sparring ground for ideas, none too precious to be challenged.

Homer shows that purpose does not erase personality; it channels it. Achilles remains ferocious, Agamemnon still pompous, but the war effort flourishes only when their formidable energies converge on a common objective: breach Troy's walls. So too in startups:

you do not neuter the maverick's creativity or the CEO's drive; you align them with a cause so clear that even grudges bend before it.

Strategic Takeaway: Vision Clarifies Every Decision

In the Achaean camp, ambiguity breeds conflict. No written charter exists; every warrior understands "honor," yet each defines it differently. Achilles measures honor in trophies and respect. Agamemnon measures it in obedience. Odysseus measures it in victory. Without a crisp, shared vision, those metrics collide.

Translate that to modern venture life: one founder prioritizes user growth, another chases revenue, a third wants technical excellence. All three goals matter, but when a sprint demands trade-offs—ship buggy but fast, or polish but delay?—lack of hierarchy breeds deadlock. A written, vivid vision imposes hierarchy. It says, for example, "We exist to make remote teams trust each other as easily as co-located teams." Suddenly speed matters insofar as it builds trust; quality matters insofar as it sustains trust; revenue arrives as proof that trust delivers value. Disputes shrink because the north star shines bright.

Homer compresses this insight into a single moment. As Hector presses the attack, the Greeks teeter at their ships. Patroclus begs Achilles: "Let me go, if you will not, into battle in your armor, so at least the Trojans may think I am you." Patroclus is not chasing personal pride. He adopts Achilles' identity to preserve the fleet—the logistical heart of the mission. When a clear vision ("keep the ships afloat so we can return home") guides the decision, even borrowed honor becomes tactical, not selfish.

Therefore the strategic takeaway for founders is simple: articulate a cause so specific that every major decision can be dropped into it like a stone into a well. If the cause is shallow, the stone clunks on visible mud and arguments start. If the cause is deep, the stone disappears without splash, and work proceeds. Vision does not remove hard choices; it illuminates them.

Action Steps

Craft a One-Sentence "Trojan War" Statement (Mission)

Your mission sentence must answer three questions the epic raises within its opening lines: Who are we? What is the struggle? Why must we prevail?

Homer answers with brutal economy: "Sing … the anger of Peleus' son Achilles that caused the Greeks untold pain, hurled down to Hades many valiant souls, and made their bodies carrion for dogs and birds." Note the structure: protagonist (Achilles), conflict (anger), stakes (suffering and death), desired resolution (none stated yet, but implied re-alignment).

For a startup, emulate the cadence:

1. **Protagonist** – Name the customer or community, not yourself.

2. **Conflict** – State the core friction they face, the thing that sparks "rage" every day.

3. **Stakes** – Quantify the cost of inaction: lost time, money, well-being.

4. **Resolution** – Hint at the better world you will deliver.

Example first draft: "We help freelance designers stop losing sleep over invoicing so they can spend nights dreaming up bold work." That single sentence identifies the hero (designers), the adversary (invoicing stress), the stakes (lost sleep, creative drain), and the victory condition (dream up bold work).

Keep pruning until every word earns its place. When you read it aloud, it should ring like the first line of an epic: rhythmic, memorable, slightly larger than life—but grounded. If team members frown or ask, "So what do we actually do?" rewrite until no such question follows.

Stress-Test It for Customer Relevance

Hector never forgets that Troy's fate includes wives, children, and "aged fathers whose knees no longer bear them." His vision is validated daily by the people he shields on the wall. Founders must validate theirs the same way: by facing customers early and often.

1. **Customer Interviews as War Councils**
   Invite early users to a live session. Read the mission aloud—no slides. Observe micro-reactions: raised eyebrows, nods, bored gazes. Ask, "Does this feel like the war you're fighting? If not, name yours." Record their words verbatim.

2. **Burn the Straw Man**
   Present three alternative missions, each emphasizing a different "enemy." Let users rank which conflict feels most acute. If your favorite sentence comes last, swallow pride; purpose belongs to the market, not the founder's ego.

3. **Quantify Pain**
   Hector measures battle momentum in spear-lengths and casualties; you measure in churn, downtime, NPS. Attach metrics to the mission: "stop losing sleep" becomes "reduce monthly unpaid invoices by 90 %." If you cannot track it, the mission is too vague.

4. **Pilot the Promise**
   Deliver a minimum viable solution that embodies the mission's core. For the designer invoicing startup, automate a single invoice end-to-end for ten freelancers. Did they actually sleep better? Call them the next morning. Listen. Iterate.

Stress-testing ends when customers echo your mission back in their own words. When a user says on a forum, "Finally, invoicing doesn't steal my 2 a.m. peace," you know relevance has clicked.

Share It Relentlessly Until the Team Quotes It Unprompted

Odysseus wields words like spears. Before any critical maneuver he "stands in the midst" and restates the goal. He tells fighters what victory looks like that day. Founders must do likewise, with frequency approaching ritual:

1. **Opening Incantation**
   Begin every all-hands with the mission sentence. Recite it, do not display it silently. Sound breeds memory.

2. **Slack Banner and Email Signature**
   Pin the sentence atop your primary communication channels. It should be harder to avoid than Achilles' reputation.

3. **Demo Days**
   Judge every feature demo by one slide: "How does this advance our war?" If the feature presenter cannot draw a direct line, the sprint misses the mark.

4. **Onboarding**
   New hires receive a physical card or digital artifact bearing the sentence. Ask them to rewrite it in their own style and share on day three. Translation deepens understanding.

5. **Performance Reviews**
   Tie individual OKRs to mission clauses. "Reduce unpaid invoices" becomes an engineering metric, a CX metric, a marketing metric. The sentence evolves into shared

currency.

The litmus test: one afternoon you stand by the coffee machine, mention "mission," and an intern finishes the sentence before you sip. That is the moment you know purpose has graduated from poster to pulse.

Bringing It All Together

Homer's first book is a masterclass in how clarity, or its absence, shapes fate. Achilles' wrath blinds the Achaeans; a sharpened sense of purpose later unblinds them. Startups need not suffer such bloodshed to learn the lesson. A single sentence, forged with discipline, tempered in customer truth, and hammered daily into the team's collective mind, can avert countless petty quarrels and wasted quarters.

Remember the pattern: pride flares when vision fades. Re-light the vision, and pride returns to productive fire. Let the "wrath of Achilles" remind you that talent without purpose is volatile, but talent aligned with mission is unstoppable.

So craft your song, make it singable, and teach everyone around you to sing it. Only then do you earn the right to march on Troy—whatever fortress of complacency your startup has vowed to overturn.

Chapter 2. Muster the Achaeans — Assemble a High-Trust Coalition

Kings of Many Cities, One Fragile Alliance

When Homer runs his famous "Catalogue of Ships," he turns what could be a dry headcount into a lesson in complexity. The list rolls on like surf against the beach: "With him came fifty ships from Pylos... From Arcadia followed Agapenor, son of Ancaeus, their chief..." The rollout is not just logistics; it is a census of rival hometown loyalties, family feuds, and private agendas. Each commander brings an accent, a dialect, and a definition of victory. The Achaean camp is therefore a prototype startup board meeting stretched across battered sand and snapping pennants. Every voice matters, every ego flares, and the ground is always shifting beneath the bronze-shod feet.

In that volatile chemistry lies the genius and danger of coalition. The force looks united when shields overlap in the phalanx, yet behind each visor is a different calculus. Ajax fights for Salamis, Diomedes for Argos, Menelaus for a stolen queen, Achilles for immortal glory. Lines of command blur unless trust braids them together. Nothing exposes the fragility faster than Agamemnon's own speech in the first assembly: "Disastrous war and painful it is to you, let us flee with our ships to the beloved land of our fathers." Panic—not strategy—tears through the ranks because the supreme leader voices retreat before clarifying intent. Homer's line "And all the people were shaken, as the great sea is shaken" shows us what happens when authority shouts but trust does not echo it. The same tremor passes through a startup when a CEO announces a pivot without groundwork; slack channels erupt, options calculators glow, recruiters circle.

The Iliad never hides the cost of mis-alignment. When Agamemnon seizes Achilles' prize, the quarrel detonates precisely because no unifying charter overrides personal insult. "You shameless, armored in shamelessness—always shrewd with greed," Achilles hurls, and an entire war effort stalls. Odysseus scrambles to patch holes, Nestor lectures, Hera meddles, and weeks slip by while Trojans regroup. Every hour of Achilles' sulk converts into Trojan market share. For a fledgling venture the analog is engineering freeze: pride halts commits, investors grow uneasy, and once-loyal early adopters drift toward an alternative product that actually ships updates.

Yet the narrative also spotlights how quickly cohesion returns when leaders earn—not demand—belief. Odysseus walks the camp, "sceptered," but he wields the rod less as a tool of dominance than of dialogue. He kneels beside each restless contingent and whispers of home, spouses, and the glory still within reach. One sailor, then a dozen, then a thousand re-shoulder spears. The lesson is blunt: relationship capital, not command charts, revives momentum. Greek kings who cannot converse as peers find their regiments curdling into rumor. Founders who dismiss coffee chats, one-on-ones, and AMA sessions discover the same rot.

Strategic Takeaway: Authority Without Trust Fractures Fast

Authority is a prognosis of what should happen; trust is the heart rate that decides whether the body moves. In Homer's world, the golden staff signifies the former, campfire stories forge the latter. Agamemnon owns ten times the territory of any ally, yet his word alone never carries the battle standard far. The Trojan front lines fall only after he apologizes, returns Briseïs, and offers lavish recompense. The apology matters less than the subtext: I need you. Authority bows; trust rises.

Modern org charts replicate the Achaean pecking order—VP, director, manager—but startups scale too fast for formal rank to encode all nuance. Yesterday's first engineer becomes tomorrow's architect; the intern who grappled with customer tickets may drive product roadmap six months later. Titles lag reality. Without habitual trust, those transitional intervals breed status anxiety and political hedging. People ask "Who approves this?" instead of "What best serves the mission?" Meanwhile a leaner competitor outruns deliberation and captures territory—users, APIs, marketing buzz—because its members already trust each other's intent.

The Iliad points straight at this peril each time Hector rallies Trojan ranks while Greek lords bicker. Standing by the Scaean Gate, spear in hand, he prays, "Zeus, grant that this day may bring an end to Achilles' insolence." Confidence flows from his posture into every shield wall. He is not supreme king—Priam is—but he enjoys unbroken trust of foot-soldiers because years in the field proved his courage. He earned credit in the only ledger that counts: shared ordeal.

Translate that to startup trenches: the head of growth who took midnight support calls earns deference when discussing retention metrics; the CTO who pair-programs through crises commands more real authority than any shiny title. Trust, like Hector's spear, is weighty yet invisible. Once it breaks, reforging is slow and public. Achilles only rejoins battle after Patroclus falls—blood payment for broken trust. A founder who hemorrhages trust often needs an equally visceral wake-up: plunge in sign-ups, churn spike, press exposé. Better to protect the bond daily than to repair it after disaster.

Action Steps

Map Critical Skills, Not Titles

Begin by asking what crafts hold the coalition together. When Homer ticks off commanders, he sneaks in competencies: Odysseus "skilled in every form of strategy," Idomeneus "strong with the spear," Machaon "the healer." The list is a skill matrix disguised as epic poetry. Build yours with equal candor. Post a living document titled "What We Actually Depend On" and populate it with verbs, not job labels: **Write performant data pipeline, close enterprise deals, translate user anger into roadmap clarity, design interfaces that a 60-year-old can use blindfolded.**

Avoid the vanity trap of stacking tasks under whichever name enjoys prestige. Maybe the founder still handles the investor pipeline—they stay—but perhaps the first-year CS grad owns **optimize load balancer failover**, an area with higher production risk. Once verbs outnumber names, clusters emerge. You see redundancy where several own the same verb; gaps glow where no one does.

Next, stack mission-critical verbs against strategic goals: *Scale to 50k DAU without latency >100ms.* Which verbs unlock that? Maybe **refactor database indices** and **redesign caching layer**. Do these verbs have owners? If not, you've located a wall breach where Trojan arrows will find purchase.

Finally, visualize the verbs as braid strands crossing project timelines. Where multiple strands converge under one name, risk looms: Achilles syndrome. Losing that person stalls multiple fronts. Plan mentor shadows or split the load early. If even mighty Achilles needs Patroclus to sub in, your unicorn engineer certainly does.

Run a "Campfire" Ritual: Each Member States Personal Stakes

Before major pushes—launch weeks, funding rounds—schedule a "campfire." It need not involve actual flames; the essence is circle, stories, and no laptops. Each participant answers three prompts:

1. **Why does this mission matter to me, personally?**

2. **What fear keeps me half-awake when I think of this project?**

3. **What one gesture of support from teammates would ease that fear?**

The first prompt surfaces intrinsic motivation. One might echo Sthenelus—"Father left unfinished glories, I mean to finish them"—translated as "My last job's product died unlaunched; I crave a win." Another quotes Neoptolemus' boast: "I will not be second," remixed as "I want my design to redefine the category." Hearing these confessions weaves empathy: you realize the finance lead burns for user delight, not spreadsheets.

The second prompt releases pressure valves. By naming dread ("I fear we will under-deliver and burn reputation"), teammates legitimize vulnerability. In the Iliad, Achilles finally voices grief for Patroclus and wrath at Hector; only then does purpose crystallize. When a QA engineer admits sleeplessness over release bugs, leadership gains impetus to adjust scope.

The third prompt converts empathy into action. One might say, "If growth shares roadmap earlier, I can craft metrics rather than scramble." Commit these asks to writing. They become small contracts—tokens of respect. As each is honored, psychological safety blooms. Soldiers fight harder for commanders who know their children's names; coders code cleaner for PMs who remember their sleeping hours.

Schedule campfire follow-ups half-way through the project and in post-mortem. Compare original stakes to outcomes. Did the fear materialize? Did support arrive? Adjust norms accordingly. Over time the ritual embeds into culture—an oral constitution binding diverse cities of code.

Rotate "Shield Bearer" Roles to Build Empathy Across Functions

Ajax carries a towering shield—wall of seven ox-hides faced with bronze—yet he rarely fights alone. Behind him darts Teucer the archer, "sheltered by Ajax's broad hide." The duo illustrates role symbiosis: one absorbs shock, the other delivers precision. Swap their positions mid-battle and chaos would ensue, yet each knows enough of the other's craft to pivot if required.

Mimic that interplay by rotating "shield bearer" assignments inside sprints. Pair engineers with CX reps on live ticket duty; have product managers shadow DevOps during deploy windows; invite marketing writers into code review as plain-language auditors. Limit rotations to a few hours per week—just enough to feel the strain and texture of another's shield.

Set three aims for every rotation:

1. **Learner articulates one respect insight.** Example: "I saw how brutal context-switching tickets are; I'll batch feature flags to reduce back-and-forth."

2. **Host gains process feedback.** Example: "Watching you struggle to trace logs showed me we need clearer error IDs."

3. **Document a joint improvement.** Even tiny tweaks—shared glossary, new hotkey script—cement the

empathy in artifacts.

To prevent role chaos, maintain a rotation roster visible to all. Odysseus would call roll before night raids; you do the same in Slack. After each cycle, host a five-minute debrief. Ask: "What surprised you?" "What will you do differently in your main role?" Let responses ripple into next OKR planning.

Over quarters this practice inoculates against silo cynicism. When marketing requests an impossible-seeming custom event, engineering now recalls the pain of explaining missing events to journalists, and hunts for a middle path. When DevOps begs for code freeze, product, having tasted 3 a.m. pager duty, pushes feature trains earlier. Trust becomes reflexive, not theoretical.

Threading the Lesson Through Culture

Coalition health is not a single project management technique; it is the air the team breathes. Homer reminds us by shifting camera angles from high councils to tent gossip to phalanx collisions. In healthy air, skeptical voices still argue, but arguments navigate toward resolution, not personal rupture. Even Achilles and Agamemnon eventually exchange gifts and oaths.

To keep the air pure, conduct a quarterly "Catalogue of Ships" ritual. Re-read the skill map, update for departures and new hires. Invite each contributor to declare, as the Achaean captains did, "Here is my domain, here is my pledge." Celebrate overlaps—redundancy means resilience—but spotlight lone wolves too. Lone capacity requires mentorship or backup.

Measure coalition quality with qualitative pulse questions:

- **If a production terror struck at 2 a.m., which teammates would you ping without hesitation?**

- **Whose job constraints do you feel confident explaining to a new hire?**

- **When was the last time a teammate surprised you with unseen craftsmanship?**

Low scores on the first indicate brittle trust; low scores on the second reveal silo ignorance; low scores on the third suggest undervalued talent.

Should metrics dip, revisit Homer's cautionary scenes: Thersites mocking kings, Ajax quarrelling with Odysseus over armor. These vignettes warn that disrespect, even from minor actors, seeds broader discontent. Address the smallest sneer fast: pin public kudos, mediate privately, uphold shared fate.

Beyond rituals, encode coalition DNA into tools. Maintain squad-level dashboards exposing cross-functional dependencies; annotate tickets with impact chains—who downstream relies on this fix? Keep retros biased toward "system over scapegoat." When blame hunts a name, remember Nestor's words: "But you young men, whom the years press upon, stand by each other." Shift focus to process gaps rather than character flaws.

Mining Further Iliadic Moments for Guidance

Consider the episode where Achilles lends Patroclus his armor. The camp has learned Achilles' shield silhouette wards off panic. When Patroclus dons it, Achaean morale skyrockets. Yet this proxy authority falters once Hector sees through the disguise. In startup translation: borrowed prestige—fancy title, interim lead, external consultant—works only briefly unless underpinned by real trust and competence. Equip stand-ins with not just the badge but the context. If a senior engineer goes on leave and a junior steps up, pair them beforehand; transfer tacit knowledge, not just files.

Another instructive passage is the night embassy: Odysseus, Ajax, and Phoenix enter Achilles' tent, each tailoring persuasion to his relationship. Phoenix invokes childhood; Ajax appeals to comradeship; Odysseus reasons with consequences. The multi-modal approach shows coalition leaders must "speak many dialects." One-size messaging misses subsets of the audience. When pushing a painful roadmap change, craft variant narratives: data-driven for analysts, vision-painted for designers, risk-framed for finance. Diverse channels reinforce trust because each stakeholder hears a voice tuned to their frequency.

Homer also portrays negative coalition archetypes worth avoiding. Paris lounges in his chamber, polishing armor but avoiding frontline hazard. His indifference erodes Trojan morale until Hector storms in and scolds: "Your people are dying in battle, and you—no blame if the men called you coward!" Startups likewise suffer when a founding member checks out during crunch. Address disengagement early, offer path back to contribution, or transition them gracefully; morale cannot carry dead weight indefinitely.

The poem closes with Priam's daring night visit to Achilles. Mortal enemies share bread and tears over fallen sons. This tableau reveals the deepest coalition superpower: humanity even in rivalry. Foster inter-team empathy, not just intra-team. Congratulate competitors on milestones, share bug bounty intel across industry; generosity nurtures networks stronger than any patent moat. Should an acqui-hire opportunity arise, existing goodwill accelerates integration.

Sustaining the Coalition Beyond the First Siege

Coalitions outlive single campaigns when they evolve governance. After Troy, Odysseus wanders, Menelaus rebuilds, Agamemnon meets tragedy at Mycenae. Each fate illustrates differing post-war trust strategies. Odysseus survives by weaving alliances—Phaeacians, shepherds, swineherds—while Agamemnon falls to household betrayal. Lesson: founders who keep authority centralized risk collapse during handover; those who cultivate distributed stewardship navigate succession.

Begin succession planning early. Rotate ownership of core systems; invite emerging leaders to board calls; document tacit "why" behind past decisions. Host "what if I were gone six months?" drills. If a function implodes under hypothetical absence, shore it up.

Refresh coalition vows at milestones: Series A close, public launch, regional expansion. Celebrate not just outcomes but behaviors that safeguarded trust. Gift personal tokens—custom email thank-yous, symbolic coins, hand-drawn avatars—to reinforce the memory. Ritual objects sustain myth; Homer embeds war stories in engraved cups and shields. Your artifacts—first 100k user T-shirts, burnt-in deploy badge—anchor group identity through the fog of sprint cycles.

Closing Reflection for the Reader

Picture the beachhead at dawn: white tents, smoke, gulls crying, thousands of warriors strapping greaves. No single king could compel that coordinated roar of sinew without the invisible mortar of trust. Every scabbard click says, "I believe you will cover my flank." Your startup, though smaller in headcount, fights battles as existential—customers' loyalty, investors' patience, competitors' encroachment.

Authority may draft org charts and issue proclamations, but only trust converts diagrams into motion. Map skills, honor personal stakes, trade shields, and revisit the covenant often. Do these things, and your coalition—like the best moments of Homer's Achaeans—will stand shoulder to shoulder, unshakeable even when the sea god Poseidon himself hurls waves at the wall. Fail, and the first quarrel will splinter resolve, scattering ambition across the wind-lashed shore.

May you muster wisely, speak frankly, and march forward under a banner every heart in the camp has sworn to defend.

Chapter 3. Reading the Omens — Deciding with Incomplete Data

Calchas the Seer vs. Real-Time Battle Chaos

The Iliad unspools its first major tactical debate when plague rips through the Achaean camp and no one knows why: bodies burn on driftwood pyres, horses founder in sand, and arrows of Apollo fall "as night over the ranks." Panic spreads faster than the sickness. Enter Calchas, "the clearest seer who knew what is, what will be, and what had been." He rises, staff in hand, yet his insight arrives wrapped in risk. To reveal the god's anger he must accuse Agamemnon of sacrilege, an act that could cost his neck. So he bargains for protection first—"Swear to defend me"—before speaking hard truth: the king must return the captive Chryseïs and pay recompense or the plague will rage on.

Calchas operates on fragments: he cannot see the whole divine calculus, only patterns in smoke, flights of birds, tremors in priestly memory. His reading proves correct this time. Yet notice how Homer frames the moment—not as mystical inevitability but as a contested data point. Agamemnon scoffs, "Prophet of evil! Never have you yet for me foretold good." The seer's forecast triggers negotiation, not obedience. Leaders weigh it against real-time chaos, political cost, moral qualms, and personal pride. Some resent the message; others cling to it because it offers an actionable theory in a fog of dying men.

Fast-forward a few books: Calchas fades from view, replaced by scouts, spies, and gut instinct. When Hector presses the assault, nobody pauses to consult entrails; commanders react to dust clouds and spear angles. They act with partial information, revise on the fly, bank on probability. Even gods toggle plans in mid-air—Hera deceives Zeus, Poseidon lends covert aid—reshaping the board before any mortal algorithm can converge. The epic becomes a symphony of incomplete data: each hero chases shards of knowledge, makes a bet, and lets consequence teach.

Start-ups inhabit the same vortex. Founders rarely enjoy full telemetry. Customer numbers spike without clear cause; servers sputter under a load model that looked safe in staging. A tweet ignites a PR storm at midnight. The temptation is to hunt for a modern Calchas—a market research firm, a machine-learning forecast, a guru thread on social media—that promises certainty. Sometimes the seer is right; more often, the signal is conditional. The key is to treat every omen as a model, not a mandate.

Strategic Takeaway: Treat Forecasts as Models, Not Mandates

Calchas offers a model: "Apollo will relent if we restore the girl and sacrifice." He does not guarantee the Trojans will exploit the lull, nor does he solve the bruised ego of a high king who feels stripped of honor. The model is only a compass pointing away from plague. Success still requires Agamemnon's concession, Achilles' temper, Odysseus' bargaining skill, and the safe sailing of a ship to Chryse's shore. Treating Calchas as an oracle would mean ignoring those human variables. Treating him as a model invites scenario planning.

Similarly, modern forecasts—financial projections, funnel conversion curves, velocity charts—encode a slice of reality under certain assumptions. They can inspire, warn, or anchor debate, but they do not override context. A SaaS team may project 10 % month-over-month growth if churn remains low; suddenly a competitor launches a free tier and churn doubles. The model flagged growth potential, not a locked destiny. Leaders must pivot before the plague of cancellations torches cash flow.

Homer drives the point home by contrasting Calchas with Hector's real-time decisions. Hector watches the battlefield like a grandmaster scanning a chess clock, yet even he misreads a critical omen: when a hawk drops a snake in front of the charging Trojans, Polydamas urges retreat, interpreting the sign as doom. Hector snarls back, "Fight for your fatherland! Omen? One omen the best—fight for your country." He rejects the snapshot and relies on momentum, and for a while he's right. Later the reversal hits when Achilles reenters; momentum proves as fickle as birds over Ida. Neither omen nor bravado guarantees outcome. Only adaptive execution—decisions revised under pressure—steers survival.

Thus, the strategic mandate: let predictions inform but never command. Forecasts are scaffolding; agility is the building. Calchas without follow-through is conversation; chaos without models is panic. The art lies in oscillating—listen, adjust, act—faster than rivals can freeze you in one posture.

Action Step 1: Red-Team Key Assumptions Monthly

Every Achaean council features at least one dissenter—Thersites heckling kings, Diomedes advising caution, Nestor drawing on age-old memory. Their dissent keeps groupthink from calcifying. In modern parlance, they red-team strategy: probing blind spots, mocking sacred cows, forcing leaders to defend logic.

Schedule a monthly red-team drill. Choose one crucial assumption—pricing elasticity, supply-chain stability, user acquisition cost—and appoint a two-person squad to break it. They operate like Polydamas reading ominous birds: their job is skepticism. Give them a week off normal duties to gather data, user quotes, external benchmarks. In the next "war council," they present worst-case narratives. Example script:

Base scenario: paid ads bring 1,000 marketing-qualified leads per month at $30 CAC.
 Red-team scenario: new privacy rules throttle tracking; CAC jumps to $90; lead volume halves.

Let core owners rebut, adjust, strengthen defences. Record decisions in a shared doc: what new safeguard or pivot did the test provoke? If the answer is "none," the team either boasts unshakeable resilience—or missed the omen. Mark for follow-up in one sprint to verify.

Rotate red-team duty across functions. The designer tasked with tanking database load will ask naive questions devs overlook. The finance analyst drafting phishing exploits for customer care will notice policy gaps. Role diversity mirrors Homeric assemblies where kings, craftsmen, and heralds all weigh in.

Key rules:

1. **No blame.** The red-team attacks ideas, not people.

2. **Time-boxed.** One week keeps skepticism sharp, not cynical.

3. **Mandatory response.** Leadership must publish the mitigation plan or an explicit rationale for inaction.

Repeat monthly. Over time the practice inoculates culture against certainty fever. You make humility habitual, like sacrificing hecatombs before a voyage—small upfront cost to avert divine wrath later.

Action Step 2: Add "Confidence Level" to Every Metric Presented

Calchas frames his reading in qualitative confidence: he is "best of seers," yet he still asks for Achilles' protection—proof he knows his signal may spark backlash. Embed the same humility into dashboards. Whenever a metric appears—ARR projection, server uptime, test coverage—append a confidence tag: High, Medium, Low. Better, attach a percentage range: 90 % confidence uptime > 99.95 %, 60 % confidence churn < 2.5 %.

How to set confidence:

- **Data volume.** More events yield higher statistical power.

- **Data freshness.** Metrics older than one market cycle degrade quickly.

- **External volatility.** If new legislation or competitor moves loom, mark uncertainty high.

- **Measurement maturity.** A/B tests with guardrails score higher than anecdotal feedback.

Use visual cues—faded opacity for low confidence—to discourage executives from treating shaky numbers as gospel. In every KPI review, start discussion with confidence drift: which metrics gained certainty, which eroded, why? The ritual paints transparency into analytics, turning dashboards from stone tablets into living scrolls with margin notes.

Borrow Homer's language to coach teams: "Let us not be blind, like Agamemnon trading lives on a rumor; let us see as Calchas sees, yet admit the mist." That invocation reminds analysts and storytellers alike that data is an omen to interpret, not a throne to kneel before.

Action Step 3: Keep a Living Log of Bets, Results, and Lessons

The epic is itself a log—twenty-four books of bets placed and recorded in dactylic hexameter. Patroclus dons Achilles' armor (bet), routs Trojans but falls to Hector (result), teaching Achilles the lethal cost of absence (lesson). Reproduction of cause and effect cements memory for future generations.

Create a "Battle Log" shared doc or database. Each entry tracks:

1. **Date & Owner**

2. **Hypothesis / Bet** ("We believe lowering free-tier limits will convert 10 % of users to paid.")

3. **Forecast Metrics** (baseline MRR, expected increase, confidence level)

4. **Intervention** (steps taken, rollout plan)

5. **Outcome** (actual numbers after set period)

6. **Retrospective Insight** (what worked, what surprised)

7. **Next Decision** (double-down, rollback, iterate)

Make brevity a virtue—bullet style, no slide decks. Link to deeper data only if needed. The aim is searchable institutional memory, not polished narrative. Encourage owners to write in first person: "I underestimated friction; 30 % churn uptick struck within 48 hours." Personal voice triggers empathy and retention.

Review the log quarterly. Surface top three wins and top three misses. Celebrate wins with rituals—digital laurel wreaths, custom emojis. Analyze misses publicly without shame. Achilles acknowledges, "Wrong I was," before rejoining battle; that admission unlocks collective adjustment. When someone repeats a historical mistake, point to the log—not to shame but to shorten the learning loop.

Over quarters the log becomes an oracle superior to any hired consultant because it is baked in company-specific context. A new PM scanning last year's log sees that feature bloat preceded latency spikes; she steers clear of repeating the pattern. The organization becomes, in effect, its own Calchas—foreseeing through accumulated scar tissue rather than entrails.

Weaving the Three Steps into Everyday Flow

Rituals fail when siloed from routine. Integrate red-teaming, confidence tagging, and battle logs into existing cadences.

Weekly stand-ups:

- Each squad nominates next month's red-team target.

- Metric owners state updates with confidence tags aloud.

- Any bet launched that week earns a quick log entry.

Monthly all-hands:

- A red-team squad presents findings; leadership responds live.

- Dashboard slide highlights metrics with declining confidence; action items assigned.

- The most instructive bet (win or fail) is retold in story form—two-minute Homeric recap.

Quarterly off-site:

- Audit the battle log for pattern recognition.

- Re-score assumptions; retire those proven stable, flag new unknowns.

- Celebrate best "seer moment"—team whose early omen reading saved major cost.

By tying rituals to paid calendars, the practice sustains beyond initial enthusiasm. Over time, company lore will cite legendary red-team calls like modern bards singing of Calchas' plague insight.

Additional Iliadic Episodes to Deepen Mastery

- **Dream Deception:** Zeus sends a false dream to Agamemnon promising swift victory. The king acts without validation, triggering disastrous initial assault. Modern corollary: unvetted executive hunch can burn runway. Lesson—demand corroboration before pivot.

- **Patroclus' Overreach:** He exceeds Achilles' instructions, chases Trojans to the gates, and dies. Even accurate early data (Trojans in retreat) must be bounded by guardrails. Define kill-switch criteria in experiments.

- **Trojan Horse (later myth cycle):** Greek stratagem uses ambiguous signal to fool defenders. Highlights adversarial data manipulation. Treat suspiciously perfect metrics or competitor gifts with forensic scrutiny.

By referencing these set-pieces in team workshops, you crystallize the attitude that every data point is context-bound and possibly adversarial.

Closing Reflection

In war as in entrepreneurship, omniscience is fantasy. Homeric warriors wield foresight like a torch in wind—flickering, partial, precious. Calchas glimpses enough to redirect destiny, yet only because leaders debate, doubt, and decide in motion. The plague lifts not by prophecy alone but by shipping a peace offering across choppy seas, by Odysseus' tactful speech, by collective willingness to pivot despite sunk cost.

Adopt that mindset. Forecast, doubt, act, learn. Keep your own omens alive yet humble. Listen to each unexpected bird cry—a metric spike, a user rant—then weigh it, tag its certainty, log the bet, and move. Repeat until your company's epic sings with victories born not of perfect knowledge, but of relentless adaptation in the face of divine uncertainty.

Chapter 4. Duel on the Shores — Positioning Against a Giant

Paris vs. Menelaus: Symbolism of Brand vs. Substance

The war for Troy ignites over a single breach of contract: Paris abducts Helen, queen of Sparta, and by doing so affronts not merely her husband Menelaus, but the honor code binding kings. Yet the Iliad quickly reframes the breach as a marketing problem. Paris, "beautiful as a god," struts in leopard-spotted cloak, a walking billboard for glamor. Menelaus, broad in chest and scarred by training, looks like every competent but unflashy product manager who grinds in silence until provoked.

When Hector discovers Paris hiding from the fight, he unleashes a tirade that is pure brand critique: "Evil-hearted Paris, fairly fashioned, woman-mad seducer — would you had never been born!" Paris' sheen cannot mask hollow performance. The defense arrives as Paris proposes single combat: his best claim is still aesthetic—spectacle over grit. "Let me and Menelaus fight for her before you all," he says, as if a duel might convert theatrics into credibility.

Menelaus accepts with a grunt: "Now we will see which man the lady follows." He knows substance wins in direct comparison, provided the audience sees the flyer and the feature side by side.

That framing turns the duel into a masterclass on positioning. Paris represents the incumbent giant, Troy: walled legacy, gilded halls, marketing myth. Menelaus embodies the upstart challenger: lean, battle-tested, clear value proposition—retrieve wife, restore honor, go home. The shoreline becomes their demo stage.

Observe the optics. Paris outfits himself in ornate armor polished like a startup deck loaded with animations. Menelaus chooses plain bronze and steady stride: "the wildcat, sure of his strength," Homer says. Paris fires the first arrow of branding by promising an epic show; Menelaus counters by promising closure. The armies gather not just for blood but for proof: which claim better serves reality?

The duel ends fast. Menelaus drags Paris by the helmet crest; Aphrodite snaps the chinstrap and spirits her favorite away, saving brand face at the cost of credibility. The Greeks howl fraud. A product that needs divine bailout is a feature that cannot scale. Audience trust shifts. Troy, the market incumbent, now carries a shadow of doubt.

Modern founders face the same optics. The market giant may flaunt Superbowl ads, glossy booths, influencer swag. A challenger cannot whine about unequal spend; it must orchestrate a duel that spotlights its comparative edge—speed, ethics, craftsmanship, price clarity—where the giant's veneer cracks. Paris sets terms he thinks favor him—a duel of spectacle—but his weakness (fragile grit) still shows. Menelaus agrees because the duel amplifies his edge (real strength). Picking that stage is the strategy.

Strategic Takeaway: Pick Battles That Showcase Your Edge

Battles cost runway. Enter only those where victory metrics align with your advantage. If your startup's moat is turnaround time, force a race. If it is transparency, force an open audit. Never fight on terrain where incumbents can smother you with volume spend.

In the epic, Paris hosts advantage in walls, archers, backup gods. Menelaus pulls him onto open sand, equalizing entourages. The duel's rules—single combat, clear outcome—strip away Trojan moats. A founder should craft similar constraints: nail a use case so narrow the leader's bloated suite feels clunky, then blast the demo.

Two filters decide worthiness:

1. **Edge Amplification** – Will the confrontation magnify what makes us special?

2. **Resource Cap** – Is the scope small enough to finish before deep pockets bury us in delay tactics?

If both pass, schedule the duel. If edge blurs or scope balloons, retreat and reconceive. Brené Brown says "Clear is kind," Homer says "Short work if God gives us courage." Same message: clarity beats bravado.

Action Step 1: Plot Competitor Feature Gaps on a "Shield Diagram"

Ajax carries a shield "like a tower," seven bullhides and a plating of bronze. Each layer guards against different threat vectors—stone, arrow, spear—which makes him nearly unassailable head-on. Yet his shield is heavy, leaving flanks slower. Your competitor's product shield is identical: overlapping layers of features, patents, brand equity, and customer inertia. Your mission is to draw the diagram, mark seams, and pinpoint where a slimmer but smarter jab lands.

How to build the shield diagram

1. **List core value claims**—every promise the incumbent makes in ads, docs, sales calls. Example for an enterprise CRM: 360-degree customer view, AI forecasting, global support, compliance.

2. **Map feature layers**—detail which modules enable each claim. Maybe AI forecasting depends on data warehouse ingestion + in-house ML studio + consultant tuning.

3. **Rate rigidity vs. agility**—assign each layer a flexibility score. Legacy code, multi-year contracts, or regulatory binds decrease agility.

4. **Identify seams**—places where one claim rests on two weakly integrated modules. Seam tension often equals latency, brittle DX, or hidden costs.

Visualize as concentric rings: outer ring is shiny marketing copy, inner rings hold grudging reality. An arrow pointing at the thinnest ring flagged "slow upgrade path" becomes your insert point.

Example

Outer copy: "World's smartest forecasting in minutes."
 Inner dependencies: data ingestion (legacy ETL), model training (manual), UI (dated). Rigidity high. Seam appears between ingestion and training; if ingest fails, model lags. A challenger offering click-to-connect ingestion and auto-training can exploit that seam.

Document findings in a shared figma or whiteboard. Annotate with real user complaints scrapped from forums: "Support ticket #3498: 'Still waiting two weeks for data mapping.'" Each complaint thickens your bullseye.

Field test the diagram

Share with pilot customers. Ask: "Does this pain resonate?" Listen for visceral affirmation. Adjust arrows until at least three reference customers declare, "If you solved that, I'd switch tomorrow." That is the Paris helmet crest you will grab.

Action Step 2: Design a Single-Feature Demo that Exposes the Incumbent's Weakness

Homer spends verses on the duel arena: trampled sand leveled, lots drawn, lambs offered. Ritual sets stakes, but duel is decided in seconds. Your single-feature demo must do likewise—strip ritual, showcase strike, end with a crowd chanting your name.

Principles of a duel-demo

- **Laser Scope** – One feature, one claim. Menelaus does not lecture on Spartan culture; he swings sword.

- **High Contrast** – Display incumbent method side-by-side. Think Paris' gold-studded spear bending against Menelaus' sturdy one.

- **Time-to-Wow < 3 minutes** – Audience attention mirrors soldiers' hush. If gods have to intervene to keep eyes on you, demo failed.

- **Measurable Outcome** – Rope around Paris' helmet crest is binary: he escapes or he doesn't. Your metric must similarly flip: data sync in 60 seconds vs. 6 hours.

Blueprint

1. **Pick the most glaring seam** from shield diagram. Suppose it is "Setup time."

2. **Construct demo script** that mirrors the incumbent flow: *open their console, count clicks: 34; open our console, count clicks: 3.*

3. **Prepare neutral environment**—raw VM or new laptop, to silence bias accusations.

4. **Invite real users** who have experienced the pain. Their gasp is testimony.

5. **Record and publish**. Menelaus' win needed the watching armies; your win needs social proof. Post the side-by-side video, annotated with stopwatch.

Handling divine bailout attempts

Paris survives by divine interference; incumbents may deploy similar last-minute rescues—bundled discounts, FUD campaigns, NDAs blocking your reference deals. Anticipate:

- **Bundling** – Answer with modular pricing that shows cost break-even in the first workflow.

- **FUD** – Publish security audits and uptime dashboards live.

- **Reference block** – Collect quotes from defectors early and anonymize until legal clears.

Design your demo narrative to mention that possibility subtly: "Even if vendor X offers credits, you still lose two weeks in data mapping." This inoculates the crowd before the giant strikes back.

Embedding Positioning into Culture

A duel is flashy, but positioning is marathon. After Menelaus yanks Paris by the crest, Helen still sits in Troy; armies still slug in dust. Therefore bake edge identification into weekly flow.

- **Monday Compass** – Kick off week by revisiting shield diagram; update if competitor announced features.

- **Midweek Demo Lab** – Reserve two hours for engineers to craft micro-experiences that shorten time-to-wow.

- **Thursday "Giant Watch" Slack** – Channel where sales drops fresh intel: pricing changes, missed SLAs, analyst downgrades. Every seam noted.

- **Friday Debrief** – Show and tell one micro-demo; rating by peer vote on "Menelaus Impact Index: 0-10."

These loops create a living radar. Your team morphs into Hector's scouts scanning ridges for Achilles' return, except here you seek sudden cracks in the giant shield.

Case Study: A Modern Menelaus Moment

Imagine a small fintech tackling a top-five bank's small-business loan portal. The bank's shield: household trust, regulatory certification, nationwide branches. Seam: approval time averages two months. Fintech edge: machine-learning risk scoring on open banking data.

Shield diagram reveals ingestion-to-decision gap. Fintech designs single-feature demo: user connects accounting software, algorithm spits credit line in 120 seconds. Banker flow is shown in parallel: PDF download, manual upload, 20 required fields. Stopwatches tick. Observer SME laughs, "That's my whole Saturday saved." Demo posted on LinkedIn hits 100k views. Next quarter, bank's SME share drops 10 %. Fintech's duel replicates Menelaus dragging Paris across sand: small guy, clear edge, public shock.

Yet note the aftermath. Bank deploys lobbyists to tighten API regulations—divine interference. Fintech, warned, had pre-filed compliance papers, turned threat into moat. Point: duel must include plan for god-level counterstroke.

Common Pitfalls: When Paris Wins after All

- **Friend Zone Demos** – You expose seam but wrap it in jargon; audience fails to feel pain. Menelaus swinging slow punches.

- **Lavish Scope Creep** – Demo tries to beat entire suite; time-to-wow balloons. Sand fills with spectators yawning.

- **Hidden Costs** – Your feature stuns but pricing obfuscates; audience suspects trick. Aphrodite warps you away at bill review.

- **Mocking Tone** – Over-trash incumbent; if demo hiccups, crowd turns. Remember Hector's scorn later haunts him.

Guardrails: rehearse with neutral advisors, stress-test on cold prospects, price transparent, and keep ego tempered: "Let results speak, we are humble Spartans."

Expanding Edge through Storytelling

After duel, embed narrative in every asset. Landing page hero copy: "Approve loans in two minutes, not two months." Case studies recount duel: stopwatch GIF. Sales decks open with quote from ex-bank client: "Felt like Paris' helmet falling off." Even internal stand-ups open with "Remember the crest"—a mantra that product must always seize the crest, visible proof of value.

Homer uses epithets—"swift-footed Achilles," "rosy-fingered Dawn"—to reinforce archetypes. Develop your own epithets for the product: "two-click import," "1-sec ledger sync." Repetition cements identity.

Preparing the Organization for Endless Duels

Paris escapes but the war continues. Incumbents spawn new product heads, new slogans, new ad buys. Build an institutional muscle:

- **Edge Library** – Confluence page cataloguing every current seam, strength, associated demo, lead outcomes.

- **Edge Owner** – Assign PM to guard each edge; if competitor closes gap, owner convenes strike team to forge fresher blade.

- **Edge Review OKR** – Quarterly objective: launch or refresh at least one edge demonstration.

Hector counts chariots at gates nightly; you count edges.

Philosophical Coda: Fighting the Right Giant

Menelaus' cause is personal and collective; retrieving Helen quenches his rage and upholds pan-Hellenic justice. Challengers sometimes mis-choose giants—fighting incumbents purely for glory, not to solve user pain. That path drifts into Paris' vanity duel: showy but hollow.

Ask:

1. **Does winning this duel make life better for users
    beyond bragging rights?**

2. **Will our product maintain edge once giant reacts?**
    (Sustainability)

3. **Does duel align with company mission sentence from
    Chapter 1?**

If any answer wavers, pivot battle choice. Glory without substance
ends in arrow flight and wind. Choose giants whose defeat
advances real value; then victory songs resonate beyond
marketing.

Closing Reflection

Homer never lets us forget that watchers matter. The duel occurs
not in secret glade but before two armies, priests, and gods.
Perception defines outcome almost as much as swordplay.
Aphrodite's rescue saves Paris physically yet damages his
reputation beyond repair. Likewise, your demo may win raw
metrics but if public sees desperation deals or hidden downtime,
trust still shifts against you. Positioning is choreography of
audience sentiment.

So craft the duel. Plot the shield diagram until weak joints glow;
sculpt the single-feature demo that cracks them; rehearse until
speed meets certainty; stage it under clear lights; capture gasps.
Accept that gods may meddle—regulation, price wars—but enter

prepared. Each honest win stacks credibility, blade by blade, until not even Olympus can obscure your edge.

March onto the sand not to mimic Paris' flair nor to bow before Trojan walls, but to stand like Menelaus: brawny, focused, convinced that substance, well-displayed, conquers glitter. When the helmet crest snaps and the crowd roars, record the moment—then get back to building, because tomorrow's giant already paces behind the ridge.

Chapter 5. Hector's Advance — Defending Core Territory

Trojan Counter-Attack Pushes Greeks to the Ships

Morning haze still clings to the Scamander plain when Hector, helm flashing "like the peak of some dark wave crested with foam," rallies his troops for a last-chance surge. Apollo has breathed fresh fire into Trojan lungs; the walls behind them thrum with women's prayers. Greeks, drained from endless shift work on the front, feel the sand shift under their sandals. Shields rattle. The familiar beat—bronze on bull-hide—mounts into a drum that drowns thought.

Hector lifts his voice: "Now drive them back to their hollow ships, burn them in flame, and let the cry of victory rise over Troy!" In that single command he names the strategic objective. The ships are not mere transport; they are lifeline, treasury, and exit plan. Torch them, and the Achaeans lose supply chain, morale, and route of retreat. Every Greek senses the calculus. Homer writes, "Panic took hold of them, a gnawing terror," as warriors glance over shoulders at black hulls beached in tight rows.

Moments later, the Trojan front slams forward. Breakthrough blossoms when Sarpedon hurls a spear that "cleaves the great hinge of the oak gate" guarding the Greek rampart. Dust swirls.

Arrows whistle. And like a lever thrown, momentum reverses months of siege: the defenders become the cornered, scraping to keep flame from seasoned timber. Men shout for water buckets, rams, anything to stave off ruin.

In startup parlance, Hector's push is a market incumbent reclaiming territory with ferocity. Maybe they slash prices, maybe they launch a copycat feature, maybe they purchase your largest channel partner. Your runway jolts into panic; the Greek shoreline is your ARR dashboard bleeding red. If the ships burn—if key revenue streams evaporate—no future expansion matters. This is the hour to defend core territory or concede the entire campaign.

Strategic Takeaway: Protect Critical Revenue Streams Before Expanding

Many founders fantasize about moonshots while their existing product lines wobble. Hector's charge challenges that vanity. A business cannot scale when its baseline cash cow is aflame. Expansion must wait until the shoreline is secure.

Greek kings learned this the hard way. They had spent resources on siege engines, ditches, and endless sorties far from camp. Yet all growth initiatives hinge on a single logistical reality: ships stocked with grain, arms, and the gold drawn from home coffers. When Hector breaches the wall, every scheme to storm Troy's high gate is put on ice. Odysseus clocks it at once, barking, "Friends, we are undone if once the fire takes the ships." He yanks warriors into a tight perimeter, focusing effort on one metric—hull integrity.

Translate that to business: if twenty percent of customers provide eighty percent of revenue, those accounts are your ships. If churn creeps into that bracket, alarms must howl. The team may dream about conquering adjacent verticals, but until retention stabilizes, new territory is false victory.

Protecting the ships buys time for later gambits. Achilles himself re-enters the war only after Patroclus dies defending the vessels. Without boats intact, even Achilles' rage would be futile—no transport home, no spoils, no legend. Founders must likewise recognize that visionary features, acquisitions, or global launches rely on current cash flow. Core customers bankroll tomorrow's heroics.

Action Step 1: Identify the "Ships" (Key Customers) You Cannot Lose

Homer wastes no breath naming every hull; he spotlights those at risk. Fire licks along the vessel of Protesilaus; Ajax plants himself beside it "like a pillar of stone." Copy the method: know which accounts matter most and who will shield them.

1. **Segment Revenue Sources by Strategic Yield**
   Pull last twelve months' receipts. Calculate net revenue retention per customer. Factor in upsell potential, referral volume, and logo gravity. Sort descending. The top cohort—often five to ten percent—are ships. Mark them red on a tracker visible to all teams.

2. **Assess Vulnerability**
   For each ship, score churn risk on variables such as feature gaps, support tickets, competitor courting, contract renewal date. A low-spend user with high evangelism might still be a ship—think Odysseus' crew steering morale. Constantly update risk flags; ignorance feeds surprise boardings.

3. **Assign Dedicated Champions**
   Every key customer gets a named Ajax: a cross-functional lead who owns success, escalation, and emotional bond. Sales closes, CS nurtures, product listens; yet the champion orchestrates consistency. Print their names on the warboard: "Ajax for ACME Corp." If champion headcount is slim, prioritize ships over all else.

4. **Run "Fire Drills" Quarterly**
   Simulate a defection attempt. Stage a role-play where competitor TrojanSoft offers a bargain. Force your champion to negotiate rescue within 24 hours—discount structure, roadmap acceleration, VIP support stack. Debrief the root causes that almost lit the hull.

5. **Signal Internal Priority**
   Just as Greeks stationed heralds near the prows, broadcast ship status in every all-hands. Celebrate renewals with ceremony—gong hit, name shouted, Slack emoji storm. Memory of salvation fuels frontline vigilance when next flame gusts.

By illuminating these accounts, you focus culture on stewardship. No one confuses vanity metrics—Twitter followers, conference applause—with the polyethylene drums of cash that keep sails patched.

Action Step 2: Build a Crisis Response Playbook with 24-Hour Fixes

When Hector hurls torch after torch, the Greek reaction is immediate. Big Ajax hoists a twelve-foot spear to knock firebrands back into the sand. Teucer stations archers to drop incendiaries mid-flight. Nestor rallies water crews. They don't convene a committee; they execute pre-memorized roles.

Your company needs the same muscle memory.

1. Stand Up a "Red Sand" Channel
A dedicated Slack or Teams room named after the blood-soaked shore. Only high severity alerts hit this feed: production outage, top customer escalation, regulatory breach. Membership includes leadership, engineering lead, CS, comms, legal. A pinned doc holds guidelines.

2. Pre-Define Critical Scenarios
Ship at Risk (key account churn alert); *Hull Fire* (major outage jeopardizing revenue streams); *Supply Blockade* (payment processor freeze). For each scenario, list:

- Primary Owner

- First 10-minute action

- Communication template to customer

- Internal status cadence

3. 24-Hour Fix Doctrine

Commit that any issue hitting a ship triggers an "all clocks pause" mode until mitigation. Engineering cancels feature work; marketing suspends campaigns that distract attention; finance clears petty cash for make-good gestures. Like Ajax, everyone grabs sand to smother sparks before they grow.

4. Root Cause & Repair Window

Within the same 24 hours, not only stop bleed but launch a repair timeline. Example: if payment failure stems from partner API, spin up backup processor and share ETA. Keep customer updated every three hours.

5. Post-Mortem Ritual

After flame dies, hold recap within 48 hours. Stick to blameless format. Log what detection missed, what comms lagged, what automation needs writing. Publish summary company-wide. Greek quarters echo with recounting of close calls; your team must do likewise to embed lessons.

6. Continuous Drills

Practice at least monthly. Trigger a faux alert at random: "Fire on Ship Athena—AWS latency spikes." Time response until fix simulated. Praise swift thinking, coach gaps. Rotating drill master ensures freshness.

With this playbook, when a real torch arcs over the parapet, reflex overrides panic. People know their lanes, scripts, fallback tools. You aim to out-pace the blaze, just as Ajax and Teucer did when they "quenched the firebrand's fury in dark sand."

Integrating Defense with Long-Term Growth

Protection is not stagnation. Greeks defend ships while still plotting Troy's fall. Likewise, safeguarding core revenue underwrites future bets. But defense consumes energy; over-rotation can harden culture into fear. Balance by linking each frontier project to a shipped metric: "This feature opens new segment **only if** NRR on core > 95 %." Gate expansion behind health of ships, and celebrate each release as both growth and proof of fortress stability.

Introduce dual metrics in dashboards:

- **Blue Line** — Core revenue retention and uptime.

- **Gold Line** — New territory metrics (product-qualified leads, international DAU).

Visualize both daily. If Blue dips below threshold, Gold initiatives auto-throttle. Explain to teams like Odysseus: "We cannot seek fresh land while the sea eats our keels." The clarity prevents frustration; everyone sees the logic.

Learning Directly from Hector's Playbook

Hector is not merely attacker; at night he checks perimeter, instructs watch rotations, orders signal fires. In essence, he guards his own core—the Trojan city—while pressing advantage. Mirrors for business:

- **Dual Buffers** — Maintain on-call roster for both offensive (feature rollouts) and defensive (bug triage) squads.

- **Moral Cohesion** — Hector implores Trojans to remember families inside walls; remind employees why saving ships matters—salaries, livelihoods, brand promise to users.

- **Agile Retreat** — When Patroclus storms out, Hector orders fallback behind Scean gate temporarily. Know when to cede low-value skirmish to reinforce vital bastion—drop a pet feature, migrate to stable infra.

Analyze Hector's eventual failure too: fatigue. Continuous assault without adequate rest leads to stretched lines, enabling Achilles' breakthrough. Translate as burnout risk. Your Red Sand channel must rotate responders, enforce rest windows.

Common Missteps When Shoreline Burns

1. **Slow Acknowledgment**
   Greeks could have ignored early torches; instead they yelled chain-of-command instantly. Founders sometimes

hide outage notifications, hoping fix precedes discovery. Customers notice. Delay correlates with trust erosion more than bug severity.

2. **Scattered Ownership**
   Multiple leaders bark contradictory orders. In Iliad, Nestor's counsel and Ajax's brawn sync because roles pre-agreed. Document single commander per crisis.

3. **Overcompensation**
   Team halts all forward motion for weeks, letting competitors reposition. Balance triage with steady drip of value—Greek archers still harry Trojans even while dousing fires.

4. **Memory Loss**
   Post-incident, company rushes back to roadmap, leaving no logs. Six months later a near-identical fire flares. Avoid by enshrining playbooks and reviewing at every planning cycle.

Building Cultural Symbols to Anchor Defensive Mindset

Greeks raise the ship-saving as myth: bards sing of Ajax's stand, Teucer's arrows. Create concrete tokens:

- **"Ajax Awards"** — Quarterly kudos for heroics that
  preserved customer trust.

- **Hull Icons** — Slack custom emoji named for top
  customers; flame overlay when they signal risk, water drop
  when saved.

- **Shoreline Wall** — Office mural or dashboard screen
  depicting current defense status.

Symbols turn abstract metrics into visceral narrative. Employees
visualize ships they defend, forging shared pride.

Closing Reflection

Hector's advance is reminder and mirror: the world does not wait
for your roadmap; adversaries—economic shocks, new entrants,
shifting user expectations—may ignite fires without warning.
Success hinges on two disciplines: knowing precisely which ships
you cannot afford to lose, and drilling a response so tight that
within a single day you extinguish flame, mend planks, and
reassure every doubter.

Anchor your organization on that shoreline discipline. Guard the
hulls that carry payroll, promise, and possibility. Only then dare to
hoist sails toward Troy-sized dreams, confident that whatever
embers the market hurls, your crew stands ready, buckets in hand,
eyes on the blue-black timber that floats your future.

Chapter 6. Patroclus in Achilles' Armor — Delegation and Identity

Borrowed Authority, Fatal Confusion

Patroclus, "gentle horseman," longs to end the slaughter rolling across the trench. Achilles, still brooding over Agamemnon's insult, refuses to fight yet cannot ignore his comrade's plea. At last he says, "Put on my glorious armor…and the Trojans will take you for me." In that single sentence Achilles gifts authority: brand, reputation, terrifying halo. Bronze greaves, plumed helm, and the great shield forged by Hephaestus become a proxy badge.

The plan works—for a time. Myrmidons roar, Trojans stagger, and momentum flips as though Achilles himself has rejoined. Yet inside the shimmering plate beats a different cadence. Achilles had warned, "Once you win back the ships, come back, do not press on to Ilion." Patroclus, drunk on victory and crowd chant, slays Sarpedon, then charges the gates. Apollo strikes him dizzy; Euphorbus spears him; Hector delivers the finishing blow. Armor clatters free, revealing the impostor. The shock ripples through both armies: a legend's shell lies empty, its wearer dead. Borrowed authority mutates into fatal confusion.

Two lessons emerge. First, delegation can multiply impact—Patroclus repels fire from the ships. Second, if delegation blurs identity boundaries, risk soars. The Trojans fight with berserk desperation once they realize Achilles is absent; Greeks reel as their talisman falls. Misalignment between symbol and substance magnifies chaos.

Modern companies reenact this drama daily. A founder hands a high-visibility project to a lieutenant, expecting stakeholders to treat the lieutenant as the founder. At first, emails get answered, decisions stick. Soon the delegate faces edge-case calls outside original remit; enthusiasm crosses guardrails; the brand mask slips. When failure erupts, observers ask, "Where was the real leader?" Trust bleeds, morale dips, and both leader and delegate wonder who owns the corpse of the mistake. Achilles mourns: "My dearest friend is dead…I urged him back, I told him once he'd beaten off the blazing Hector to come back to the ships." He realizes delegation delivered tasks, not protective clarity.

Strategic Takeaway: Delegate Tasks, Not Identity

Delegation should offload execution while preserving unmistakable authorship lines. Achilles needed to send "Patroclus the deputy," not "Achilles 2.0." Leaders must separate **role** (temporary authority to decide within scope) from **identity** (permanent source of credibility and accountability). The moment Patroclus donned the full regalia—with the god-wrought shield that only Achilles should wield—he stepped over the boundary. Teams viewing a deputy must know, in their bones, where the deputy's decision stops and where the leader's begins.

Consider the contrast with Odysseus' ship. When he naps, he assigns the rudder to trusted Helmsman Perimedes, but leaves cloak and scepter beside himself. No sailor mistakes Perimedes for Odysseus; yet the ship sails true. Authority delegated, identity intact.

Apply this to product development: a VP of Engineering chairs a release, but the CTO's vision remains explicit, documented, and sign-posted at each checkpoint. Customers can escalate to CTO if stakes escalate; engineers know where architectural veto resides. Confusion dissolves, even under pressure.

Action Step 1: Create a "Skin-in-the-Game" Matrix for Delegated Projects

Before armor exchanges hands, write a matrix clarifying four dimensions for every key player:

1. **Scope of Decision** – Exactly what battlefield does the delegate own?

2. **Symbolic Markers** – Which badges (title, email sign-offs, Slack access) transfer, which stay?

3. **Risk Share** – How much consequence—bonus, reputation, equity—rides on delegate's performance?

4. **Come-Back Gate** – What explicit condition triggers escalation back to original owner?

How to Build It

- **List Projects in Rows**: Each epic or campaign.

- **List Roles in Columns**: Original Owner, Delegate, Stakeholders.

- Fill cells with bullet answers. Example:

- **Scope**: "Own feature alpha rollout to beta customers only."

- **Symbols**: "Delegate signs 'for the product team,' but CTO remains final approver on press quotes."

- **Risk Share**: "Delegate's quarterly OKR bonus weighted 40 % on NPS delta."

- **Come-Back Gate**: "Escalate if latency >200 ms for more than 30 min or if legal flags compliance."

Keep this matrix visible—pin to project board, link in calendars. When someone asks, "Can Patroclus pursue Trojans to the gates?" the matrix answers: Scope ends at ship rampart.

Enforce Review Rituals

- **Kick-off Review** – Walk through matrix live; invite challenge.

- **Mid-sprint Check** – 15-minute sanity check: Are we inside scope?

- **Post-Launch Audit** – Score each dimension; adjust for next iteration.

Over time the matrix conditions culture. Delegation becomes a contract, not a costume swap. People learn to respect identity lines and still step boldly inside delegated arenas.

Action Step 2: Hold Post-Mortem to Separate Role Clarity from Blame

Achilles' first impulse after Patroclus' death is self-recrimination: "I let my dearest friend go forth alone." Yet Greek commanders soon analyze contributing factors—Apollo's ambush, aborted rally, armor weight. They articulate what decision sat with Achilles (restrict pursuit), what with Patroclus (heed limit), what with chance (godly interference). This distinction lets them adapt tactics rather than spiral into vendetta.

Modern post-mortems must emulate that clarity exercise. The goal is to refine delegation mechanics, not scapegoat. Structure:

1. **Timeline Reconstruction** – Chart signals, decisions, outcomes.

2. **Decision Ownership Tagging** – For each decision, tag Owner per matrix.

3. **Gap Analysis** – Identify where delegate acted beyond
    scope or lacked authority.

4. **Systemic Improvement** – Draft process tweaks: escalate
    earlier, clarify come-back gates, calibrate risk weighting.

5. **Emotional Debrief** – Space for participants to express
    grief, frustration, or pride without crosstalk.

Record learnings in a living doc titled *Achilles-Patroclus Ledger*.
Each new delegation references prior entries. This compounding
knowledge inoculates against repeating identity confusion.

Illustrative Modern Scenario

Company: SaaS analytics startup.
Leader: Founder/CEO, charismatic, customer-facing.
Delegate: Director of Product riding herd on crucial enterprise
migration.

CEO, overloaded, tells Director: "Take my calendar slot with
BigRetail Inc. Pitch roadmap, they'll think it's from me." Director
presents, nails tactical asks, then casually promises a bespoke
data lake integration the CEO never vetted. BigRetail hears
Achilles-level guarantee. Weeks later, engineering balks; delay
erupts; BigRetail threatens churn. Cost: $1 M ARR risk, morale
slump.

Matrix Autopsy

- Scope misdefined: "Pitch roadmap" mutated into "commit new feature."

- Symbolic confusion: Signing authority on product scope remained ambiguous.

- Come-Back Gate missing: No rule to ping CEO before promising >4-week dev.

- Risk share lopsided: Director faced internal blame; CEO faced customer rage.

Fix

- New matrix mandates exec approval for feature commitments exceeding sprint backlog.

- Director receives explicit "spokesperson" badge but not "signatory" badge.

- Escalation Slack channel: #armor-check.

Avoiding the Patroclus Trap: Best Practices

- **Partial Armor, Full Brief** – Delegate only the gear necessary. Patroclus could have worn Myrmidon crest without the god-forged shield. In business, lend authority on price negotiation, but keep signature line reserved.

- **Shadow Rule** – Leader shadows first key meetings silently, withdrawing once delegate proves alignment.

- **Echo Back** – Delegate paraphrases mission boundaries in writing before launch: "I understand we stop at the ships; I will not chase beyond."

- **Public Acknowledgement** – Leader intro's delegate to stakeholders: "Patroclus leads the assault within defined perimeter; ultimate accountability remains with me." External clarity reduces rumor shock when identity discrepancies surface.

Cultural Component: Pride and Humility

Delegation thrives on humility from both sides. Achilles' pride kept him from the battlefield; Patroclus' pride drove him past limits. Implement programs:

- **Humility Huddles** – Bi-weekly 10-minute reflection of top brass: state one area you do **not** know.

- **Delegate Diaries** – Slack thread where delegates share near-misses, fostering transparency over bravado.

- **Armor Ceremony** – Symbolic hand-over item (token, Slack emoji) returned upon project completion, signifying impermanence of borrowed power.

These rituals anchor identity awareness in collective psyche.

Closing Reflection

Achilles lends power; Patroclus wields it with brilliance, then blurs into fatal overreach. The lesson is not "never delegate" but "delegate like Odysseus steers," with tether lines and mutual respect. Leaders must encode guardrails so authority travels far without fracturing identity. Delegates must honor scope, wielding borrowed armor as trustees, not heirs. When both disciplines hold, armies repel assault, products ship on time, and legends live—not as empty bronze rattling on sand, but as thriving partnerships in which every actor knows exactly whose name rings behind each triumph and each risk accepted.

Chapter 7. The Shield of Achilles — Product as Story

Hephaestus Forges a Cosmos on Bronze

Homer pauses the roar of battle to follow the lame god Hephaestus into his volcanic forge, where bellows "pant in quick succession" and bronze runs "like living water." At Thetis' request the smith shapes a new shield for Achilles, five layers deep, edged in triple gleaming rim. Yet the miracle is not the metallurgy; it is the narrative impressed upon the face. Concentric zones depict the whole rhythm of mortal life: **a city at peace** with weddings, law courts, dancers; **a city at war** with ambush, siege, and the gods weighing fate; **tilled fields, vineyards in harvest, shepherds fending wolves, young men and women whirling in a circle dance**, and finally **the encompassing Ocean River** that girdles everything. When Hephaestus lifts the finished work, it "flashes far, as the moonlight."

The shield contains an encyclopedia, but it does not read like one. It reads like a worldview laid bare: creation is struggle and celebration intertwined, bounded by mystery. Achilles straps it on and strides into the fray, carrying not just defense but a portable myth of why he fights. Each Trojan who sees the shield glimpses a story that dwarfs personal quarrel—cosmos against chaos.

Modern products likewise project stories before users dive into features. The first five seconds on a landing page, the tactile heft of a phone in palm, the micro-copy of an error state—all speak louder than spec sheets. A product too often is treated as an inventory of capabilities, yet customers treat it as a symbol that affirms how they see the world or how they hope the world might be. Hephaestus teaches founders that shape and tale merge: when you release something, you offer a vision of order, value, and belonging. Features are bullet points beneath that banner.

Strategic Takeaway: A Product Conveys Worldview Before Features

Imagine if Hephaestus had etched only plaques labeling *materials: 80% tin, 20% copper; weight: 55 lb.* The shield would still stop spears, but no bard would sing it. Its power lies in framing—users do not ask "What O-ring tolerance?" first; they ask "Does this fit me? Does it harmonize with my sense of purpose?" Apple understood this with the iPod's "1,000 songs in your pocket" pitch. They displayed a worldview: music as freedom. Transistor count came later.

When early Myrmidons cluster round Achilles' new gear, they are, in effect, unboxing a product reveal. They gasp because the shield interprets existence. That interpretation shapes their morale. Similarly, in SaaS, a dashboard's color palette and default metrics tell customers what matters. Choose churn as center tile, you depict survival tension; choose daily gratitude score, you depict community flourishing. Either way, story seeps first, function follows.

Therefore founders must craft narrative coherence intentionally. If a brand claims transparency yet hides pricing behind demos, dissonance cracks faith. If the app's onboarding promises calm and then bombards with red exclamation badges, trust frays. The worldview must thread consistently from hero statement to success state.

Action Step 1: Audit UI/UX for Narrative Coherence

1. Surface the Implicit Plot

Gather a cross-functional triad—designer, PM, copywriter. Screen-record a cold user journey: the homepage visit; sign-up; first data entry; first alert. Replay in silence. What emotional beats surface? Awe, confusion, relief, anxiety? Which metaphors dominate—journey, cockpit, playground? Write verbs shouted implicitly: *explore*, *command*, *heal*, *defend*. This uncovers the living plot your product currently tells.

2. Compare to Intended Myth

Recall Chapter 1's mission sentence. Does the journey embody that quest? If you promise "turn experts into superheroes," does the interface hand a cape or handcuffs? Incongruity marks points where story and surface mis-mesh. For each mismatch, label **clash**. Example: mission values calm, but splash animation jitters; clash flagged.

3. Inspect Symbolic Elements

Hephaestus used concentric rings; you use typography, whitespace, iconography. Ask: What does each symbol whisper? A lock icon next to knowledge base may suggest secrecy not openness. A skeuomorphic paper plane for "send" may align with playful narrative or undermine professional gravitas. Keep elements that reinforce myth; refactor those that muddy it.

4. Trace Micro-copy Tone

Patroclus on the shield is silent, yet dancers sing; courts buzz. Similarly, tooltip voice sets stage. Collect every snippet: empty-state jokes, error apologies, loading quips. Lay them in one document and read like poetry. Does cadence stay consistent? If "Hm, something went wrong!" sits next to "Critical failure: contact admin," tone gyrates. Pick one register—formal, cheeky, scholarly—and commit.

5. Score Coherence

Create a simple three-column rubric: **Screen**, **Aligns (Yes/Partial/No)**, **Fix Idea**. Walk through high-traffic flows. Where "No," prioritize sprint cards. Limit improvements to small purposeful gestures: color re-grade, sentence swap, icon rotate. Massive redesigns may be overkill; often narrative unification is nuance, not upheaval.

6. Validate With Naive Eyes

Recruit three users unaware of rework. Have them narrate feelings while using the product. If their adjectives echo your mission adjectives, coherence improved. If not, iterate. Like Greek soldiers glimpsing farmland on the shield and saying "It reminds me of home," your users should voice recognition of deeper promise.

Action Step 2: Ship a "Mini-Epic" Release Note That Frames the Why Behind Every Change

Homer devotes an entire book to descriptive unveiling before Achilles actually uses the shield. Likewise, founders often push updates without storytelling, losing momentum. A **mini-epic** release note is not a laundry list; it is a guided tour that stitches changes into narrative progress.

1. Choose an Arc

Select a frame—e.g., "Winter Offensive," "Harvest Release," "Second Voyage." Title sets expectation and metaphoric milieu. Tie it back to cosmic worldview: if product is about empowerment, maybe "Torchlight Update."

2. Structure in Scenes

Rather than bullet features, present **scenes**: *Scene 1: The Gateway Opens* (fast sign-up); *Scene 2: Allies Gather* (team invites), etc. Each scene ends with a one-sentence user benefit couched in emotional outcome: "Now your crew forms in seconds, so you sail sooner."

3. Embed Direct Quotes

Homer peppers shield narrative with sounds: "boys whistling," "girls in fine linen." Borrow this by quoting user feedback that spurred change: "I felt lost tracking orders," wrote Maya, so we birthed **Journey View**. Real voices authenticate motive.

4. Visual Companion

Provide a stylized illustration—GIF or static—mirroring shield craft. Maybe concentric circles of UI modules. Keep resolution light to load swiftly; links to hi-res storyboard optional.

5. Heroic Stats

Conclude with a glance at measurable victories: "Beta squad saw 24 % faster close rates." Keep numbers concrete but few; they serve as spears flashing, not spreadsheets.

6. Rites of Acknowledgment

Name the internal Hephaestuses: "Armor carved by @lin-frontend and @zhao-svg," plus contributor emojis. This deepens myth of craft, reminds users that artisans, not faceless walls, forged tools.

7. Call to Quest

Finish on invitation: "Stride forth and test the shield. Tell us where it bends." Provide feedback portal link. Mirrors Achilles taking shield into live fire and discovering edge cases.

Publish mini-epic across changelog blog, in-app modal, and email echo. Track open rate, click-through on try-new-feature CTAs; compare to prior plain-text notes. Typically engagement leaps when story precedes spec.

From Myth to Metrics: Measuring Narrative Impact

Storytelling is not fluff; it shapes adoption. Instrument analytics before and after narrative overhaul:

- **Activation time**: drop signals clarity.

- **Feature discovery depth**: narrative coherence often increases exploration.

- **Support ticket tone**: run sentiment analysis on inbound queries; stories reduce confusion, change frustration lexicon from "broken" to "don't understand."

- **Referral quotes**: tally how many advocates mention values rather than features ("It just makes me feel organized").

Plot trends. Even Achilles' shield would topple if too heavy; ensure narrative weight uplifts, not encumbers.

Pitfalls to Avoid

1. **Lore Overload** – A twelve-page release scroll may bore; keep verses short. Hephaestus chiseled silence between vignettes—space for imagination.

2. **False Symbolism** – Do not mask absence of improvement with purple prose. If feature backlog thin, better deliver small but real fix than wax mythical.

3. **Inconsistent Sequels** – A mini-epic sets precedent; next release must maintain quality or risk anticlimax. Plan cadence: maybe quarterly epics, bi-weekly humbler notes.

4. **Design Dictatorship** – Forcing narrative coherence by executive fiat can stifle experimentation. Provide compass, not cage; allow playful side missions so long as core myth stands.

Case Vignette: A Financial App Re-Shields

Background: FinTech "LedgerWave" struggled with adoption—users praised security but churned in onboarding. Mission: "Empower creators with financial calm." Yet first screen sported dark graphs and alerts.

Audit Findings: Narrative clash—visual gloom contradicted "calm." Micro-copy scolded missed receipts.

Fix: Reskinned in airy whites, subtle blues; replaced "Alert! Reconcile now!" with "Let's balance your creative flow." Introduced concentric dashboard inspired by Achilles' shield: center ring shows cash runway (life), middle ring invoices due (conflict), outer ring long-term goals (peace beyond war).

Mini-Epic Note: Titled "The Quiet Forge," walked readers through craft metaphors, quoted a sculptor who said, "Numbers used to scream at me—now they hum."

Outcome: Activation +18 %, support tickets -25 % over two months, Net Promoter Score rose. Users wrote tweets: "LedgerWave feels like breathing space." Worldview transmitted, features secondary.

Extending the Shield — Future-Proof Storytelling

Hephaestus built cosmos but left empty center for Achilles' reflection. Your product story should allow user to insert self. Provide customization: theme toggles, modular cards, personal progress arcs. Maintain brand pillars yet adapt orbit.

As company grows, the shield narrative may need extra rings: sustainability commitments, community marketplace. Add layers thoughtfully, preserving symmetry. Annual story summit—cross-departments gather, review shield diagram, decide if new ring belongs or dilutes. If mission shifted, reforge entire surface; risk heavy technical debt analogous to brittle bronze if you rivet patches.

Remember Hephaestus was invited. Listen to customers—Thetis equivalents—who plead for change born of pain. Craft emerges from empathy.

Closing Reflection

When Achilles marches with the new shield, even those unmoved by strategy feel surge: a hero attended by song of creation itself. Likewise, when your product lands in a user's hands and instantly explains not just *how* but *why*, loyalty kindles. Build features with rigor, but cast them inside a worldview bright enough to orient and deep enough to house human aspiration. Let every pixel, word, and process echo the story. Then, when market battles rage, customers will carry your emblem not merely as tool but as testament—bronze that reflects a cosmos they choose to believe in.

Chapter 8. Embassy to Achilles — Negotiation Under Pressure

The Long Walk to the Myrmidon Tents

Greek hopes sag as Trojan fire licks the ship prows. Agamemnon faces the cost of his pride and calls counsel. "I was blind, and Zeus took my wits," he concedes, sending Odysseus, Ajax, and old Phoenix to beg Achilles back. The trio trudge through moonlit sand, heavy with gifts—tripods, war stallions, Briseïs untouched, oaths of future glory—yet heavier with the task of bending a will "like iron cold-forged." Their march is a master-class in high-stakes negotiation: time scarce, stakes existential, counterpart furious. Homer's lines tighten the mood: "They came to the ships and huts of the Myrmidons, and they found him delighting his heart with a clear-toned lyre." Achilles is calm; the embassies are desperate. Every word must land.

Three Voices, Three Value Keys

Odysseus: The Pragmatist
He leads, kneeling first. "Most glorious son of Peleus," he begins, invoking status yet steering swiftly to incentive: "Take pity on the Greeks… the gifts are countless." He lists horses, gold, seven cities—tangible levers of ambition and legacy. Odysseus frames

return not as surrender but as profit: a larger stage for Achilles' fame.

Phoenix: The Mentor

Phoenix stands next, eyes blurred with age. "I made you what you are, dear child," he reminds Achilles, telling the parable of Meleager who refused to fight until it was too late. Phoenix appeals to identity as dutiful son and student. His currency is memory, belonging, paternal pride.

Ajax: The Peer

Last speaks Ajax, sparing rhetoric: "Achilles, son of savage Peleus… the men honor you, yet they drown in spears." He presses honor-bound camaraderie, not gifts or nostalgia. In Ajax's view, Achilles' truest self is warrior for brothers. He ends blunt: "If you are set upon going home, go. Others will fight on." That threat of social isolation tests whether Achilles' need for tribe outweighs his wrath.

Three ambassadors, one mission, three different maps of value. None insult Achilles; each tries to unlock a distinct door in his psyche. Negotiators facing hardened resistance must do the same—speak to values, not egos. Ego is brittle and loud; values run silent and deep.

Strategic Takeaway: Tailor Arguments to Values, Not Egos

Ego says "I am greatest," value says "I protect my own" or "I seek immortal renown." Odysseus offers more glory, Phoenix offers timeless respect, Ajax offers the fellowship of equals. Achilles listens because each pitch speaks to a value he regards higher than public flattery. Even so, he refuses—proving that any value can be ranked. His scale, that night, places personal justice above all.

Modern parallel: an investor, a key hire, or a regulator may seem immovable. Their refusal often masks an unmet value: security, autonomy, ethical alignment. Offer conference badges or higher comp and fail; speak to the missing value and doors crack. Founders err when they assume everyone prizes the same coin—valuation, headlines, speed. Negotiation is anthropology under time-pressure: decode tribes, stories, fears.

Action Step 1: Build a Persuasion Grid—Incentives, Fears, Identity Triggers

1. **List Stakeholders in Rows** – counterpart, allies, silent veto-holders.

2. **Incentives Column** – what tangible wins move them? Cash, market access, cycle time, job security. For Odysseus it was cattle and gold.

3. **Fears Column** – what disaster keeps them up? Reputation loss, regulatory flare, missed quarter. Phoenix weaponized the fear of regret.

4. **Identity Triggers Column** – which self-story must negotiations affirm? Hero, caretaker, innovator, guardian.

Ajax tugged at warrior-brother identity.

Populate the grid through research—public speeches, social posts, back-channel chatter. Then craft message bundles that strike two columns minimum: incentive + identity, or fear + incentive. Rehearse delivery so tone matches trigger: rational stats for incentive, anecdote for identity, risk scenario for fear.

During live talks, mark responses: smile, frown, note-taking. Update grid in real time. Over sessions, clusters emerge—signals to double down or drop. The grid becomes living HUD, like Argus eyes on Odysseus' shield.

Action Step 2: Rehearse "Walk-Away" Scenarios to Strengthen BATNA

Achilles could refuse because he had an alternative: sail home, live long though obscure. That Best Alternative to a Negotiated Agreement gave leverage. The ambassadors' BATNA was defeat. Effective negotiators enter with clear walk-away line and contingency actions.

- **Define Red Lines** – scope, timeline, concessions beyond which you exit.

- **Draft Post-Exit Narrative** – how you message collapse to team, market.

- **Line Up Resources** – if funding talks fail, pre-secure bridge loan; if hire declines, ready next candidate.

- **Role-play Exit Announcement** – speak it aloud; note emotional surge. This makes leaving a viable option, not a bluff.

Practice deepens calm. Odysseus knew, should Achilles refuse, they must fortify ramparts and find another moral spark. You too must script the morning after. Paradoxically, visible readiness to walk raises perceived power, nudging counterparts to accommodate before cliff edge.

Pitfalls and Guards

- **One-Size Pitch** – Agamemnon tried sending gifts list alone earlier; Achilles spurned. Customize or perish.

- **Moralizing** – Calling the opponent wrong rarely shifts them. Phoenix teaches by story, not scold.

- **Hidden Agenda Leak** – If Odysseus had sold Achilles on gold while plotting his exile, trust would crater. Align words with bona fide offer.

- **Over-Attachment** – Ajax's blunt exit line is risky yet healthy; know when commitment warps into neediness.

Modern Case Vignette

A SaaS startup needs Fortune-100 integration. Counterpart CTO values **technical elegance**, fears **vendor lock-in**, holds identity as **open-source champion**. Grid says: offer transparent APIs (incentive), roadmap to donate modules upstream (identity), uptime SLA with escape clause (fear antidote). Negotiation shifts from price trench to shared philosophy. Deal signs at modest ARR but unlocks marquee logo.

If talks had obsessed on discount alone—ego of "best deal"—CTO would disengage. Values trumped vanity.

Closing Reflection

The embassy fails in the moment—Achilles stays out—yet seeds of persuasion sprout later when Patroclus falls. Achilles recalls Phoenix's warning and Ajax's plea; the values they touched flare. He re-enters war, not for Agamemnon, but for the value of loyal companionship. Negotiations often germinate slowly; value-based appeals linger, ripening under new context. Speak to what matters most, document offers, sustain respect. Pressure can bend wills, but resonance with core values is the only force that bends them without breaking future alliances.

Chapter 9. Night Raid — Unconventional Advantage

When Lamps Go Out and Plans Turn Fluid

A low moon hangs over the Trojan plain. Campfires sputter to embers, sentries shuffle in half-sleep. Yet in the Achaean trench Odysseus' eyes still glitter. "My heart within me stirs," he whispers, scanning shadows. The line belongs to Diomedes minutes later—"My father, Tydeus, was no sluggard, even under starlight"—but the spirit already crackles between them: action when everyone else assumes pause.

Homer stages Book X almost like a heist film wedged into epic poetry. Agamemnon worries that Trojan fires "blaze a thousand strong" while Greeks tremble. Instead of ordering mass maneuvers, Nestor suggests a stealth probe. Two volunteers step forward: Odysseus, master of cunning, and Diomedes, breaker of helmets. They do not crave committee approval. They need freedom, minimal gear, and a slice of darkness.

Armed with sword, bow, and a prayer to Athena, they cross no-man's-land, capture the Trojan scout Dolon, strip intel like lock-picks—positions of chariot troops, passwords of Thracian sentries. Then they creep farther, slit twelve Thracian throats, and drag King Rhesus' glittering horses back to camp. Dawn reveals the haul. Greek morale rockets; Trojans awake decapitated of fresh reinforcements. The entire night's work was executed by a two-person squad in perhaps three hours—no fires, no armor walls, no corporate decks.

The genius of the episode is its asymmetry. While bureaucratic power centers sleep, a micro-team rewrites advantage curves. Homer underlines smallness: "Two against thousands," yet leverage surges through speed, stealth, and precise intel. The lesson cannot be clearer for startups contending with giants or for incumbents fearing insurgents. Under cover of complacency, nimble actors can carve decisive slices of value.

Strategic Takeaway: Small Teams Can Out-Maneuver Lumbering Foes

Most enterprises mirror the Trojan camp at night—layers of process, siloed watchlines, gates built for daytime show, not nocturnal agility. A pair of intentional disrupters can traverse these blind spots undetected because they move outside expected rhythms and rulebooks. Odysseus and Diomedes win not by brute force but by exploiting slack: unguarded horses, dozing sentries, leaders convinced dawn is the only hour of consequence.

For founders, the analogy lands threefold:

1. **Temporal Asymmetry** – Attack when markets assume stasis (weekends, holidays, downturns).

2. **Information Asymmetry** – Acquire insight the dominant player would never deem worth spycraft—customer gripes,

fringe API hooks, forgotten regulatory footnotes.

3. **Focus Asymmetry** – One precise deliverable (horses) outweighs dozens of partial objectives (storm the wall, capture city). Small teams with single outcomes beat massive orgs diffused across OKR matrices.

Even established companies must nurture their own night-raid cells before competitors do. Bureaucracy smothers curiosity; experiment squads keep it breathing.

Action Step 1: Schedule Quarterly "Black-Ops" Sprints for Radical Experiments

Black-ops sprint: a five-to-ten-day cycle where a micro-team (two to four people) operates under relaxed governance to test ideas too risky, weird, or dissenting for mainstream roadmap. Rules echo Book X.

1. **Select Mission Brief**
   CEO or product head drafts one provocative question:
   "How might we onboard 10× faster with zero support touch?"
   "What revenue stream lives in data exhaust we currently discard?"
   The brief is minimal—objective, guardrails (no legal breach), success metric.

2. **Volunteer Crews Only**
   Post brief on an internal board. Anyone can raise hand.
   Limit to four seats; scarcity sparks urgency. Diversity
   trumps hierarchy—pair senior architect with fresh grad,
   marketer with SRE.

3. **Shield from Routine**
   Team receives calendar immunity and a private Slack
   channel. Meetings drop to nil except daily fifteen-minute
   stand-ins. Provide budgets equal to one percent of
   quarterly R&D—enough for paid pilots or third-party hacks.

4. **Night-Raid Principles**

   - **Stealth**: No status decks until debrief; parallel work
     continues unperturbed.

   - **Consequence**: If POC works, leadership commits
     within forty-eight hours to resource scale-up or
     explicit kill.

   - **Code of Honor**: No dumping unreviewed code into
     prod, no brand-risk PR stunts. Like Diomedes
     sparing Greek watchfires, respect allies.

5. **Debrief at Dawn**
   Sprint ends with a thirty-minute demo: problem, hack,
   data, next ask. Data dictates yes/no. Even "failure" reveals
   guardrails. Document insights, move on.

Implement a scorecard tracking black-ops freshness (ideas attempted), conversion rate (POCs promoted), and morale spike (self-reported energy). Leaders who skip a quarter see stagnation; like Greeks ignoring night scouts, they invite enemy surprise.

Action Step 2: Reward Calculated Risk, Document Both Wins and Flops

Odysseus and Diomedes earn physical prizes—the horses of Rhesus—and public praise. Equally, if they had died, the army would recount their courage. Homer immortalizes both victory and cost. Modern orgs, however, often applaud only successes, burying experimental tombstones under NDAs. That asymmetry breeds risk aversion: why volunteer if failure erases credit?

Build a balanced ritual:

1. **Victory Tokens**
   Tangible, communal symbols (custom enamel pin, Slack "Horse" emoji) bestowed on successful black-ops squads. Tokens accumulate; display counts on profile like battle laurels.

2. **Valiant Flop Archive**
   Company wiki hosts a *Hall of Noble Failures*. Each entry logs hypothesis, method, result, cost, and takeaways—written by the squad in first person. Searchable by tags. Celebrate fiercest lessons at all-hands.

3. **Risk-Weighted Bonus**
   Allocate pool (say 5 % of R&D payroll) to experiments.
   Bonus splits irrespective of outcome, provided squad
   followed sprint protocol and produced actionable insight.
   Finance thus quantifies learning as capital good.

4. **Storytelling Slots**
   At every quarterly meeting, one victory story and one flop
   story share equal stage time. Ensure applause decibel
   parity. The narrative of failure normalizes daring; the
   narrative of triumph shows path.

5. **Post-mortem Templates Mirroring Book X**
   Ask squads to answer: *What darkness did we enter?
   Whom did we interrogate? What did we bring
   back?*—Dolonesque framing anchors memory.

Dark-Run Ethics: When Unconventional Becomes Unacceptable

Night raids risk moral overreach. Diomedes kills sleeping
soldiers—effective, yet ethically gray. For businesses, black-ops
must never rationalize vandalism, privacy invasion, or
manipulation. Codify a *Red-Line Charter*:

- No exploitation of security holes without disclosure path.

- No scraping data that violates terms or user consent.

- No misrepresentation of identity in competitor research.

Embed a compliance liaison (like Athena's invisible escort) reachable for rapid consult without red tape. Darkness should veil tactics, not integrity.

Case Study: Data-Ghost Team at a Mid-Market CRM

Situation: Giant competitor bundles AI forecasting; our mid-market CRM lags.

Black-Ops Brief: "Create proof that small-sample forecasting beats incumbent on quarter predictions for SMBs."

Crew: Two data scientists, one ex-customer-success lead.

Tactics: Pulled anonymized support transcripts, trained lightweight language model overnight; built plugin to surface 'sentiment drift' as leading churn signal.

Outcome: In five days, presented dashboard predicting churn 30 days earlier than competitor's model at 1/20th compute. Leadership green-lit 3-month sprint.

Valiant Risk: Model flagged false positives at scale; pilot stalled. Yet transcript labeling pipeline now informs sentiment-based upsell, generating 6 % revenue uptick. Black-Ops credited though headline goal pivoted.

Scaling the Night-Raid Culture without Chaos

The paradox: institutionalize unconvention without turning it conventional. Safeguards:

1. **Cap Parallel Raids** – Limit to two active squads. Scarcity keeps aura special.

2. **Rotation Policy** – Nobody raids twice in a year; spread daring mindset.

3. **Narrative Continuity** – Give each raid codename referencing epic: Project Dolon, Rhesus, Moonblade. Embeds mythic DNA, keeps memory alive.

4. **Sunlight Checkpoints** – Board gets quarterly one-pager summarizing objectives, compliance checks, resource spend. Transparency to prevent skunkworks drift.

From Tactical Surprise to Strategic Edge

Night raids rarely win wars outright. Yet they tilt momentum, buy breathing room, demoralize the foe, and generate institutional myth. More crucially, they feed the main army with accurate maps and stolen assets. A black-ops sprint's highest value may be the dataset, partner insight, or user narrative it uncovers—not the prototype.

Channel insights back into core roadmap. Hold **Integration Councils** post-raid: product managers pick through spoil list; engineers assess tech debt; marketing spins story; legal secures patents. Knowledge flows; the army evolves.

Closing Reflection

Homer gives the night raid only one book, yet its pulse echoes across the whole epic: Achilles re-enters to defend the ships Odysseus and Diomedes helped save; Trojans lament the unguarded horses. In modern ventures, small audacious squads will not replace disciplined operations, but they will safeguard relevance when market giants grow complacent. Train them, shield them, celebrate them, and daylight will find your company holding a prize the bigger forces never saw coming—a set of gleaming horses ready to pull you forward into the next blaze of opportunity.

Chapter 10. Return of Achilles — Re-aligning Talent After Conflict

"The Black Tide of Grief Came Surging Over Achilles"

Patroclus lies on a bier, face covered, armor stripped by Hector, and Achilles folds over the body "with both hands tearing his hair." Homer dwells on the rawness: "A sudden, sharp shudder went through him … his noble heart in agony." Grief is not a side-story; it resets the epic. Every Greek eye returns to the silent giant whose wrath once froze their own courage. They fear what form that grief might take.

The camp watches two outcomes wrestle inside Achilles:

- **Rage** — a furnace that could scorch friend and foe alike.

- **Renewed Purpose** — the possibility that the furnace will smelt his talent back into service of the cause.

At first rage dominates. Achilles vows to eat Hector's flesh, to abandon burial rites until vengeance. But grief also cracks his isolation. He allows Thetis to cradle him, he lets comrades wash Patroclus' corpse, he speaks to Agamemnon without insult. Homer marks the pivot with a single line: "So reconciled, the two set forth." Rage becomes fuel, but purpose grips the reins.

Start-ups endure similar crucibles. A key engineer quits, a product launch flops, an investor bails. Talent reels. Leaders must transmute emotional heat into kinetic alignment before it melts the culture. Ignore the grief and morale decays; indulge the rage and blame spreads like wildfire. The craft is to harness emotion without letting it rule—exactly the discipline Achilles learns at the funeral pyre when he commands, mourns, and ultimately steps onto the plain with new clarity.

Strategic Takeaway: Harness Emotion Without Letting It Rule

Emotion is information. Achilles' sorrow signals irreplaceable bond; his rage signals violated justice. Likewise, a designer's tears over scrapped mockups hint at meaning invested, a salesperson's fury at lost deal reveals stake. Leaders err when they either muzzle these currents ("be professional") or let them dictate agenda ("we pivot because we're angry"). Instead, channel them.

Achilles achieves this by ritual:

1. **Naming the Loss** — He calls Patroclus "my other self," publicizing depth.

2. **Honoring the Bond** — He organizes funeral games, converting mourning into community.

3. **Setting a Boundary** — Only after rites does he return to war. Emotions have their hour, then objectives resume.

Modern teams need analogous structures: retrospectives that let frustration surface, ceremonies that honor overtime sacrifices, and clear signals of closure so focus can reset. Emotion then becomes momentum, not undertow.

Action Step 1: Run a "Why We Fight" Workshop After Setbacks

When a release fails or market shifts, schedule a 90-minute session within 72 hours—soon enough to catch honest feeling, late enough that initial shock subsides.

Phase 1 – Story Circle (30 min)
Everyone answers two prompts in turn:

- *Name what hurt.*

- *Name what still matters.*

Stick to first-person. No solutions yet. The aim mirrors Achilles addressing Patroclus' body: "I said I would bring you home, yet here you lie." Raw admission fosters shared reality.

Phase 2 – Value Map (30 min)
On a whiteboard, facilitators cluster the "what still matters"

phrases: user trust, creative joy, financial security, peer respect. Draw connecting lines; notice convergences. This recreates the Greeks circling Patroclus' pyre, forging common ground.

Phase 3 – Commitment Draft (30 min)
 Translate value clusters into one to three battlefield statements:

"We fight to prove craftsmanship trumps schedule slippage."
 "We fight so freelancers get paid on time, even in recession."

Participants vote with dots. The top statement becomes rallying cry for next quarter. Document it, share company-wide, echo at stand-ups. By articulating meaning amid setback, the workshop re-aligns talent with mission.

Action Step 2: Offer Psychological Safety Sessions to Process Burnout

Achilles' grief is processed aloud—talking with Thetis, with the embassy, with Briseïs. The camp gives him space instead of demanding immediate performance. Provide your team with structured safety nets.

1. Confidential Debriefs
 Set recurring one-on-one slots with a trained coach or in-house counselor. Employees may vent privately, sparing team channels from emotional overflow.

2. Peer Vent Pods
 Trios meet weekly for 20 minutes; rule: share one stressor, one

win, offer listening not fixing. Rotating pods spread empathy across org.

3. Burnout Radar Survey
Monthly pulse: rate energy, clarity, support. Any score <3 triggers proactive outreach. Publish anonymized heatmap.

4. Recharge Tokens
Each teammate gets two "Patroclus Days" per year—short-notice mental-health days, no questions. Normalize use by leadership taking them first.

5. Grief-to-Growth Workshops
Quarterly 2-hour sessions where facilitators teach cognitive reframing: identify loss narrative, rewrite as learning narrative, share. This mirrors Achilles forging new purpose from Patroclus' death.

Safety sessions are not perks; they are structural airlocks preventing the decompression sickness of sustained high stakes.

Integrating Emotional Intelligence into Daily Ops

1. **Opening Temperature Check**
   Start sprint planning with round-robin: one word state-of-mind. Simple, fast, flags tension.

2. **Ritualized Closure**
   End major milestones with brief applause and a "moment

of exhale"—a toast, a meme wall, a collective stretch.
Signals permission to release adrenaline.

3. **Visible Leader Vulnerability**
   When founders narrate their own stumbles—like Achilles
   admitting "Fury has brought me grief"—they model safe
   expression. Record these in internal blogs.

4. **Conflict Mediation Protocol**
   If dispute escalates, mediator convenes 15-minute triage:
   clarify facts, feelings, future plan. Prevents simmering
   resentments from becoming Achilles-Agamemnon scale.

Pitfalls to Avoid

- **Over-Therapy** — Endless circles stall progress; set
  timeboxes.

- **Tokenism** — Offering yoga while pushing 80-hour weeks
  breeds cynicism.

- **Hierarchy Silence** — Managers skipping sessions
  invalidate norm.

- **Emotion Suppression** — "No drama" policies drive issues
  underground, where they warp morale.

Balance humanity with execution: feel, process, act.

Modern Parallel: Post-Layoff Re-alignment at SaaSCo

SaaSCo cut 15 % staff after funding crunch. Survivors felt guilt and anger. Leadership ran a "Why We Fight" workshop:

- Losses named: friends gone, fear of extra workload.

- Values mapped: product impact on small-business owners, team craft pride.

- Commitment drafted: "We fight so mom-and-pop shops thrive without MBAs."

Psych safety plan introduced: weekly vent pods, optional therapy stipend, transparent roadmap. Within two months, feature velocity recovered, Glassdoor sentiment rose 0.6 points, churn dipped. Emotion harnessed, not silenced.

Closing Reflection

Achilles shows the arc from hopeless rage to purpose-driven surge. Teams that brave emotional surf rather than dam it reclaim momentum. Teach people to name pain, frame meaning, and support one another until the heat of feeling re-tempers talent into sharper steel. Then, like the son of Peleus striding in new armor, they can return to the marketplace—fierce, focused, and unbroken.

Chapter 11. The Scamander River — Scaling Dangers

When the Battlefield Rebels

Achilles has just ripped through the Trojan front like wildfire. "As a lion comes on cattle," Homer says, "so Achilles stormed." Limbs litter the dust, armor clanks like panicked bells, and the son of Peleus drives fleeing men straight into the reed-choked bends of the Scamander. Corpses heap so high that the river itself gags. Water eddies red; fish scatter; banks collapse under the weight of iron and flesh.

Suddenly the god inside the current rears up. "Stop, great Achilles!" Scamander roars, "clog my lovely pools no more. I am choking in the filth of slaughter." Achilles curses back—"River, river, show me respect!"—and hurls yet more bodies. The god's patience snaps. He swells his coils, "rearing like a green-mane stallion," and lunges to drown the hero, sluicing mud and uprooted willows. Achilles scrambles, cries to Zeus, and only divine intervention from Hera and Hephaestus—who scorches the river to steam—saves him.

The scene is visceral warning: unchecked growth, unchecked momentum, can provoke backlash not from rivals but from the very system that once carried you forward. Achilles uses the river as throughput channel for his success metric—enemy kills per hour—until the channel revolts. In modern terms, you scale a product, a campaign, a data-harvest pipeline so fast that infrastructure, regulators, public sentiment, or the planet itself rebels like Scamander flooding the plain.

Strategic Takeaway: Growth Can Trigger Systemic Backlash

"Always strive for growth" is a startup catechism. Yet the Iliad shows growth has thresholds. At small volumes the river washes blood away; at extreme volumes it transforms into adversary.

For companies, the same inversion curve appears:

- A clever referral loop delights early adopters; at scale it looks like spam.

- A data-hungry recommender improves relevance; at scale it alarms privacy watchdogs.

- Fast-fashion output thrills investors; at scale it chokes landfills and invites legislation.

The danger is believing yesterday's supportive current will forever bear heavier loads. Instead, each growth stage alters the environment, sometimes enough to weaponize it against you. Achilles learns too late that success metrics can destabilize context; the river he dismissed becomes a lethal competitor.

Action Step 1: Map Externalities (Regulatory, Cultural, Environmental)

Every scaling plan must draft an *Externality Map*—a living artifact that tracks ripple effects beyond direct P&L. Build it in three passes.

Pass 1 – Regulatory Perimeter

List jurisdictions touched by expansion: data residency, labor law, advertising standards. Note pending bills, activist momentum, and agency backlogs. Achilles mocked local geography; don't mock local law. Mark each cell green (clear), amber (watch), red (barrier).

Pass 2 – Cultural & Social Sentiment

Probe narrative climate. Are journalists framing your tech as empowerment or extraction? Does TikTok satire target your brand voice? Gather qualitative pulse: social-listening dashboards, focus groups, academic papers. Remember Scamander's first hint was a low murmur of eddies before the tidal rise; early sentiment murmurs matter.

Pass 3 – Environmental & Infrastructure Limits

Chart energy draw, water use, landfill impact, server latency, carbon footprint. Overlay supplier fragility—rare metals, single-source APIs. Ask not, "Will it break at 10×?" but "Who suffers if it breaks?" Scamander flooded adjacent farmland, not just Achilles.

The map converts invisible currents into visible risk. Review monthly; assign owners to each hotspot—legal, Comms, DevOps.

Action Step 2: Install "Kill Switches" for Runaway Campaigns

Kill switches are pre-coded brakes that halt or throttle activity if metrics exceed safe bands—before the river floods.

1. **Define Guardrails**
     Volume: max emails per user per week; *Throughput*: max server calls per second; *Spend*: max bid on ads per region.

2. **Embed Automation**
     Use feature-flag services or circuit-breakers in infrastructure. If parameter > threshold, system deactivates module, sends alert.

3. **Human Escalation Protocol**
     On trigger, page cross-functional "River Board": ops, PR, legal. Decision in <30 min—resume, throttle, or pivot narrative.

4. **Dry-Run Drills**
     Quarterly simulate runaway—flip flag in staging, verify alarms, check dashboards show "Scamander rising."

5. **Public Contingency Copy**
     Pre-draft comms: blog post acknowledging halt, reasoning, next steps. Achilles lacked a statement; you won't.

Kill switches signal maturity to investors and regulators. Paradoxically, they speed innovation by letting teams push harder, knowing brakes exist.

Modern Parallels

Ride-sharing surge pricing improved driver supply until storms saw 8× fares and media fury. Uber now caps multipliers—an automated kill switch.

Crypto NFT minting jammed networks; high gas fees punished ordinary users. Future drops use dynamic block allocation, throttling mint speed.

DTC mattress ads saturated podcasts; listener backlash forced spend caps. Companies now pace impressions per listener ID.

Each case mirrors Scamander: environment—press, chain, audience—pushed back.

Integrating Backlash Awareness into Culture

- **Launch Gate Checklist** — No feature ships without "River Row" section: what if 100× usage tomorrow?

- **Reward Cooler Heads** — Bonus metrics include "prevented crisis events," not just growth curves.

- **Mythic Memo** — Circulate a one-pager retelling Scamander as cautionary allegory. New hires learn the river lesson Day 1.

Closing Reflection

Achilles survives, but singed, wiser. He has seen a non-human stakeholder revolt. When your company surges forward, ask: who or what is the river in our path? Map it, respect it, embed safeguards. Then growth can flow wide without turning on itself, and you need not beg the gods to quench an avoidable flood.

Chapter 12. Duel at the Gates — When Founders Must Face Off

"Hector, strongest spear of Troy, stood fronting fate; Achilles, swiftest of all Achaea, flashed like a star in night's black vault."

The Iliad's crescendo is not a massed charge but a person-to-person reckoning. Two armies freeze, holding collective breath, while their champions stride into an arena no wider than a city gate. "My time has come," Hector whispers, feeling the weight of Troy's years upon his shoulders. Achilles answers with silence, letting the new armor Hephaestus smithed do the talking. This is the final mile of competition, stripped of delegation, dashboards, or diplomatic weave. Brand, logistics, and luck have carried each side to the threshold, but the gate will swing on founder energy alone.

In start-up life, M-and-A talks can stall, market dominance can hinge on keynote day, or a lawsuit can threaten to define a category—moments that collapse to one founder confronting another under klieg lights. Board members advise, PR teams prep, yet the multiplier is personal. How you wield your own strengths, manage triggers, and tell the story of that confrontation determines whether the gate opens in triumph or slams in ruin.

Strategic Takeaway: The Final Mile of Competition Is Founder-to-Founder

During long campaigns, companies compete through product, distribution, culture. But when stakes crystallize—antitrust hearing, live televised debate, talent poaching feud—the crowd stops parsing feature lists and focuses on the two human faces that personify each mission. Homer underscores this with ritual. Achilles chases Hector thrice round Troy's walls until gods fix the moment; crowds perched on ramparts peer "as men watch fiery star fall." Decision compresses to personal courage, clarity, and narrative control.

Two insights surface:

1. **Leaders Carry Symbolic Gravity**
    Achilles' very presence rearranges troop morale; Hector's fall shatters Trojan spirit. Likewise, investors mark valuation shifts when a founder tweets or testifies. Your persona, history, and body language become proxy metrics for entire balance sheets.

2. **Personal Blind Spots Decide Outcomes**
    Hector's fatal error isn't slower swordplay; it's misreading Achilles' unbroken resolve. Founders often stumble not because product falters but because ego overestimates stamina or underestimates opponent's conviction.

Therefore you must prepare as rigorously for personal showdowns as for any roadmap—track psychological KPIs, script comms, rehearse pressure scenarios.

Action Step 1: Prepare a Personal Leadership Scorecard — Strengths & Triggers

Just as COOs model cash runway, founders must model *self-runway*—inner resources that power public duels.

1. Inventory Core Strengths

Write five verbs you consistently perform at elite level under stress. Achilles' include *close distance fast*, *read feints*, *radiate intimidation*. Yours might be *story-tell numbers*, *spar ideas live*, *absorb hostile questioning*. Support each with anecdotes and data: investor note, press quote, NPS from team Q&A. Strengths are your reliable weapons; polish them.

2. Map Known Triggers

Hector breaks when Achilles reminds him of past shame. Identify stimuli that hijack your calm—being called naïve, aggressive, derivative; interruptions; mis-facts about origin story. Note physiological cues (pulse spike, throat tighten) and default reactions (over-explain, sarcasm). Triggers left unmapped will knock sword from hand at gate's hinge moment.

3. Stress-Test in Simulation

Set up "red-team interviews" quarterly: colleagues role-play rival founder, hostile reporter, or skeptical regulator. They prod triggers;

you practice pivot. Record video, analyze posture, filler words, escalation spiral.

4. Track Recovery Lag

After each skate-fire interaction measure minutes to baseline clarity. Gradual reduction shows resilience training. Achilles loses Patroclus and rages days; by duel day he channels fury into crisp execution.

5. Establish Ritual Pre-Fight Kit

Outline 60-minute prep template: breathing cadence, mantra, playlist, final message to team. Stick to it before board calls, pitch contests, deposition cross-exams. Ritual counters chaos.

Document scorecard in a private file. Update after every major confrontation. Make it living telemetry of founder fitness.

Action Step 2: Script Crisis Communications That Humanize, Not Glorify, Rivalry

Homer refuses pure villain/hero binaries; he lets both champions show tenderness—Hector with Andromache, Achilles weeping for Priam. Startup duels likewise captivate when narratives honor shared humanity. Over-villainizing the rival rebounds; courts, press, and recruits distrust caricature.

1. Draft Dual-Perspective Narrative

Prompt	Achilles-Voice Example	Hector-Voice Example
———	———	———
What does the rival genuinely seek?	"Hector fights for his city's children."	"Achilles defends fallen friend's honor."
Where do our missions intersect?	"Both envision fewer years of pointless siege."	"Both cherish excellence in craft."

Use this empathy map to frame public statements. It prevents "us vs. monsters" tropes.

2. Choose Tone Pillars

Decide three adjectives your message must project—*relentless, transparent, respectful.* Review every tweet, op-ed, testimony against them.

3. Pre-Write Key Scenarios

If rival announces lawsuit – release within two hours a 200-word statement: "We respect their contributions; here's data; we'll resolve constructively."
If live debate gets heated – prepared closing: "Competition reveals how much progress matters to all of us."

Store templates with legal/PR clearance.

4. Spotlight Team Not Trophy

Post-duel win: highlight shared research, customer stories, industry uplift. Achilles, after victory, hosts funeral games, honoring community, not flaunting trophy alone. Avoid chest-thumping that triggers regulatory or talent backlash.

5. Provide Off-Ramp for Rival

Leave door ajar—acqui-hire, standards consortium, charity pledge. Humans remember grace; Hector's father kneels and Achilles returns corpse, earning lasting honor.

Duel Mechanics: Translating Homeric Beats to Founder Showdowns

Iliad Beat	Startup Parallel	Execution Cue
Three circuits around Troy — testing nerves	Pre-deal negotiation rounds	Maintain pacing, don't rush concessions
Athena tricks Hector (deceptive ally)	Rival arrives with misleading metrics	Verify third-party data before pivot
Spear toss misses, second hidden in shield	Unexpected feature reveal in live demo	Prepare backup showcase
Final pledge before gods	Public code-of-ethics signing	Show principled stance
Achilles drags the body — PR crisis	Over-celebration on social	Engage counselor quickly; restore dignity

Studying these rhythms lets founders anticipate emotional beats and pre-decide responses.

Integrating Duel Readiness into Company Fabric

1. **Founder AMA Rhythm** – Monthly unscripted sessions with staff to test clarity under fire.

2. **Ethics Council** – Cross-team group monitoring rhetoric; alerts when language slips from firm to spiteful.

3. **Mindfulness Stipend** – Company funds meditation or coaching for leaders to shorten trigger loops.

4. **Debate Club** – Quarterly Oxford-style debates on hot product issues; trains respectful sparring.

These structures distribute duel literacy throughout culture; future execs learn to face gate moments with poise.

Closing Reflection

Achilles wins the duel but loses a measure of his own humanity, prompting later acts of reconciliation. Founders, too, must recognize victory costs. Design scorecards to keep identity grounded, craft communication that elevates ecosystem, and remember that beyond every gate stands not just market share but mutual story. "He thought of his own father," Homer writes, when Achilles finally releases Hector's body—proof that in the

loneliest mile of rivalry, what endures is the capacity to see the
other side and still choose honor over vanity.

Chapter 13. Ransom of Hector — Win-Win Exits

The Midnight Walk of a King

Night shrouds the Trojan plain when Priam, frail monarch of a besieged city, slips out through the Scaean Gate. He rides in a mule cart, guided by Hermes in disguise, carrying no spear—only treasure: "twelve robes, twelve cloaks, twelve blankets, twelve white mantles, twelve doublets," bars of gold, a glittering cup. And one silent plea. His purpose is unthinkable: to ask the man who killed his eldest son for the corpse.

Achilles broods in his hut, the body of Hector still lashed to the chariot outside. The hero's heart is hot ash. Yet when the old man steps over the threshold, Achilles startles as though a ghost appeared. Priam kneels, "embracing Achilles' knees," and utters a line that tears the war open: **"I kiss these hands that killed my sons."** He adds another, softer blade: **"Remember your own father, godlike Achilles… and pity me."** Achilles' anger cracks; tears course down both faces. "He gently pushed the old king from his knees," Homer writes, "for a reverence of his white head took hold of him."

The exchange is the earliest literary template for a humane exit negotiation. One side holds absolute advantage; the other offers wealth but aims for dignity. By appealing not to pride but shared humanity—and by offering value beyond the battlefield—Priam secures the return of Hector's body and an eleven-day truce for burial rites. Achilles, in turn, regains moral balance and the admiration of friend and foe. The war will resume, but a durable pocket of peace has been carved and both sides exit the moment with reputations enhanced.

Modern mergers, acquisitions, or market withdrawals mirror this eerie stillness. After relentless competition, the victor must decide: crush the rival completely or craft a win-win off-ramp that preserves assets, communities, and goodwill. History shows the latter scales better. AOL–Time Warner ignored it and imploded; Disney's purchase of Pixar honored legacy and flourished. Even in venture shutdowns, founders who handle layoffs with grace find talent boomerangs back to their next idea. Priam and Achilles teach that reconciliation is not weakness; it is compound interest on victory.

Strategic Takeaway: Even Victors Need Reconciliation for Durable Value

A purely extraction-based exit—where the acquirer strips people, patents, and leaves cultural rubble—resembles Achilles dragging Hector's body round the tomb. It satisfies ego, frightens onlookers, but seeds long-term resistance. Nike founders still cite how Adidas tried to strangle them in court; Slack grew partly because enterprises resented heavy-handed tactics from incumbents. In economic rivers, resentful currents return.

Achilles grasped this the moment he felt the king's tears soak his hands. "He felt desire to weep for his own father," Homer says, "and taking the old man by the hand, gently he pushed him away, for fear that his grief might rise to frenzy." He chooses empathy over domination, preserving his legend and ensuring safe passage for Trojan elders who would, one day, shape post-war commerce in Asia Minor.

For founders, a graceful exit—asset sale, acqui-hire, shutdown, or even massive victory lap—requires three design principles:

1. **Integrative Planning** – Outline how two cultures, codebases, or user communities will mingle without fracture.

2. **Legacy Stewardship** – Offer rituals, memorials, or spin-outs so that blood, sweat, brand equity live on.

3. **Narrative Co-Authorship** – Share the microphone when proclaiming what comes next; former rivals become future endorsers.

Fail at any and resentment festers—regulators sniff, employees leak, brand karma sinks.

Action Step 1: Draft Post-Deal Integration Charters Before Signing

Before ink dries, convene a *Charter Council*—five to seven leaders from both entities, including at least two frontline makers. Charge them with producing a four-part document:

1. Purpose Alignment

State the merged mission in plain language. Achilles declares, "Come, let us put our griefs aside," signaling new phase. Your charter might read, "By joining, we accelerate carbon-neutral logistics for every SME by 2027."

2. Non-Negotiables

List red-lines: "Remote-first stays remote," "Open-source repo remains public." Priam specifies burial rites length; Achilles consents. Non-negotiables anchor trust.

3. 90-Day Integration Roadmap

Sketch thematic sprints: tech stack audit, brand style merge, benefits harmonization. Avoid Gantt sprawl; keep bullet milestones.

4. Ritual Calendar

Plan symbolic acts: logo reveal party, codebase 'first commit' together, remembrance slideshow of legacy product screens. These mirror the eleven-day truce—time-boxed space to salute the past.

Sign the charter simultaneously with legal docs. Publish internally the next morning. Stakeholders then see a humane scaffold, not conquest rubble.

Action Step 2: Offer Legacy Options to Acquired Teams (Brand Museums, Alumni Networks)

People bond deeply to logos, color palettes, even quirky 404 pages. When those vanish overnight, motivation plummets. Offer tangible ways to honor that heritage.

Brand Museum
 Spin up a lightweight microsite or physical wall in HQ displaying milestone screenshots, first swag, conference photos. Add narrative captions from original team. Invite ex-employees to contribute artifacts—like Priam bringing heirloom cups. Quarterly happy hours in front of the museum let new hires absorb lineage.

Alumni Network
 Create Slack or Discord titled "House of Hector"—opt-in space for alumni of acquired firm. Provide job boards, AMA calls with leadership, stipend for meet-ups. This keeps talent goodwill; they become evangelists, not critics.

Open-Source Freeze Frame
 If you sunset a product, open-source select modules under permissive license. Pin a disclaimer: "No further updates; preserved for community learning." The gesture echoes Achilles promising Priam safe passage: code free of legal snares.

Scholarship or Grant
 Allocate portion of deal proceeds to sponsor annual scholarship in the old brand's name. Sentiment generates press halo and demonstrates values continuity.

These actions cost little yet convert potential bitterness into alumni pride.

The Ritual of Hand-Back

When Achilles lifts Hector's body from the cart, Homer lingers on tactile detail: he orders bath water warmed, cloths laid, oils massaged into skin. He strips away dirt so Priam doesn't faint at first sight. In corporate exits, mirror this care:

- **Data Hygiene** – Audit user migration scripts; guarantee no losses or privacy breaches.

- **Customer Comms Staging** – 48-hour email cadence: announcement, FAQ, timeline. Support leads available on Zoom AMA.

- **Team Exit Interviews** – Encourage honest feedback; document lessons for future deals.

Respect in small hand-offs signals respect in larger fates.

Pitfalls That Reignite War

1. **Trophy Display Syndrome** – Publishing rival's logo in defunct list sparks outrage. Avoid dragging bodies.

2.   **Delayed Rituals** – Push integration charter to post-close, and chaos fills vacuum.

3.   **Binary Narrative** – Media framing as "winner crushes loser" inflames regulators. Counter with joint op-ed.

4.   **Benefits Cliff** – Cutting insurance or equity vesting day-one breeds ex-employee revolt on Glassdoor. Schedule soft landings.

Remember, Achilles' worst moment is dragging Hector; his redemption comes in returning him. Choose redemption first.

Closing Reflection

As dawn breaks, Priam steps back onto his mule cart, bearing Hector's body swathed in "soft purple robe." Achilles watches, feeling lighter. The war's finale is still unwritten, but a doorway to future trade, healing, and myth now exists. Your company's victories will likewise resonate longest when you exit battles with opponents dignified, partners unscorched, and your own humanity intact. Durable value grows where reconciliation waters the soil scorched by competition.

Chapter 14. Trojans Plot in the Night — The Cycle Never Ends

"And in each man's heart hope stirred again, whispering that tomorrow would be different."

Troy is shrouded in uneasy silence. Hector is gone, Priam weeps, but the city's towers still stand, and torches still burn in every corridor. Homer closes the **Iliad** without the fall of Troy, yet he seeds the next disaster: restless captains debate, craftsmen hammer new gates, and talk circulates of a great wooden horse—a "gift for Athena"—that will roll through those same gates and open them from within. The poem ends, but the cycle of rivalry and renewal does not. "Such thoughts they traded in the night," Homer says of the Trojans, foreshadowing the stratagem that will undo them.

So it goes with markets. A company celebrates victory—Series C, global launch, record ARR—only to discover in the hallway murmurs of disruption; a slender competitor with an unconventional model; a shift in regulation; a sudden platform change. Success contains the seeds of its own vulnerability. The walls that kept rivals out can trap arrogance in. For founders, the lesson is stark: **market advantage decays; plan for renewal, or be breached from the inside.**

Strategic Takeaway: Market Advantage Decays; Plan for Renewal

When Homer has the Trojans drag the Horse through their own gates, he makes a brutal point: the threat you least expect is the threat you invite. Victory dulls vigilance. The Achaeans, who once battered the ramparts unsuccessfully for ten years, succeed the moment they switch tactics—gift over force, stealth over siege. By dawn, Troy's walls are useless, and firelight flickers off polished shields marching straight down cramped streets.

Today's incumbents stumble similarly. Kodak buried digital prototypes. Nokia laughed at touchscreen toys. Blockbuster turned down Netflix's offer. They did not fail from lack of talent or assets; they failed because cycles turned and their gaze remained trained on yesterday's attackers instead of tomorrow's Trojan Horse.

Hence, founders must bake renewal into culture long before metrics slip. Doing so requires explicit rituals that force leadership to stare at uncomfortable possibilities and resource experiments that could cannibalize cherished lines of revenue.

Action Step 1: Schedule an Annual "Trojan Horse" Review

What it is.
 A deep-dive off-site where executives, ICs, and a rotating "outsider quorum" spend forty-eight hours asking one question: *If someone toppled us in the next eighteen months, how would they*

do it? The outsider quorum may include a moonlighter in your ecosystem, a journalist, a student, even a former competitor—anyone with license to blaspheme against sacred cows.

Why it works.
The Trojans held city-wide festivals to celebrate their perceived security. A Horse review flips the festival into autopsy-before-death: examine blind sides while still healthy. By formalising paranoia, you blunt the shock when disruption appears.

How to run it.

1. **Gather Pre-Mortems.**
   Weeks before, every functional lead submits a two-page memo titled "How We Die." Finance imagines margin squeeze scenarios; engineering imagines unforced downtime cascading PR disasters; product imagines dreadful churn after a free AI clone. The goal is brutal candour.

2. **Map Attack Vectors.**
   In plenary, facilitators tape wall charts labelled *Cost, Convenience, Experience, Status, Regulation.* Teams pin their memos under each vector. Patterns emerge—maybe three separate memos flag a cheap open-source alternative creeping up.

3. **Role-Play Incursion.**
   Split into red teams. One plays insurgent founder, another regulator, another disgruntled superuser. They craft a

one-year plan to breach your moat. Rules: no apocalypse fantasy; tactics must leverage existing tech or plausible policy shifts.

4. **Present Breach Narratives.**
   Red teams pitch live. Leaders listen without rebuttal, as Priam should have listened when his chief priest warned against accepting the Horse. An observer panel grades each scenario for realism and impact.

5. **Distill Counter-Motions.**
   After sleep, reconvene and choose three highest-risk breaches. Draft "counter-motion one-pagers" assigning research to verify risk, propose defences, or even embrace the idea as internal experiment.

6. **Publish and Track.**
   Summaries ship to the whole company. Each quarter, an operations analyst updates status—has anyone in the world advanced on the breach vector? If yes, escalate. If no, review again next year.

Cultural notes.
– Rotate facilitators; new eyes = new heresies.
– Reward bluntness; give a "Cassandra Award" to the harshest truth-teller.
– Archive outcomes; the folio becomes an institutional memory, like epic bardic verse warning descendants.

Action Step 2: Allocate 10 Percent Budget to Moonshots That Could Kill Your Core Product

"If we don't build it, enemies will."
Odysseus built the Horse precisely because a brute-force siege plateaued; radical shape-shifts win when incremental hacks stall. Dedicate a tenth of your spend to internal Trojans—projects whose success might cannibalise old cash cows but future-proof relevance.

Framework for Moonshot Portfolio.

1. **Define Kill-Switch Hypothesis.**
   Each moonshot answers: "What critical assumption about our business would this invalidate?" Example: *Assumption—users will always choose premium UI SaaS over command-line tools.* Moonshot: a CLI version for power users that is free, open source, and riskily efficient.

2. **Time-Box and Stage-Gate.**
   Twelve-week exploratory build → six-month advanced proto → pivot or merge. Funding rolls over only if validated learnings exceed threshold.

3. **Separate Brand Skin.**
   House moonshot under a neutral label to gather unbiased feedback; like the Horse bore Athena's sigil, not Greek flags. This prevents user confusion and internal antibodies.

4. **Success Metrics Divergent from Core KPI.**
   Where core business tracks MRR, moonshot may track

DAU of non-paying tinkerers. Protects projects from premature ROI hatchets.

5. **Umbrella Governance.**
   Quarterly Moonshot Council (a sub-board) reviews: kill, amplify, or spin out. Publicise decisions so team witnesses that risk is tolerated, not buried.

6. **Re-Entry Path.**
   If moonshot proves world-class, integrate gracefully: dual-pricing tiers, feature gating, brand migration plan. If it fizzles, publish post-mortem—lessons feed next horse.

Budget maths.
Ten percent looks steep. Yet Alexander outspent entire city-states on scouts before each battle. Insurance against irrelevance is cheaper than rebuilding after collapse.

The Permanence of Cycles

Homer emphasises cycles: "So the old man slept, and the young kept watch." Even as Trojan walls rise, seeds of ruin germinate. Greece too will later see her league splinter. Likewise your startup may crest, IPO, then fight complacency. Accept cycles; prepare in the up-swing, not the trough.

Ritualise vigilance, invest in self-disruption, document the warnings sung by your own Cassandras. Then when a strange wooden gift rolls up to your gate—be it new tech, rule, or viral meme—you will know to scan its belly with X-ray eyes before dragging it inside. And should you choose to invite it in, you'll do so on your terms, with escape hatches and renewal scripts already drafted.

Thus the epic closes, torchlight on faces both hopeful and afraid. But your company's story remains open-ended—spinning, evolving, forever one bright cycle away from either conquest or catastrophe. Guard the gates; nurture the horse.

Conclusion. Your Iliad — Closing the Scroll and Picking Up the Pen

1. From Wrath to Afterglow: Distilling the Loop

"Sing, O goddess, the anger of Achilles…" With that thunderclap Homer launches an engine that never stalls: **anger → action → consequence → meaning**. Every scene in the epic, and every chapter you have just read, rides that flywheel.

- **Anger.** A spark of emotional friction. Achilles feels dishonor; Agamemnon feels slighted; Hector feels duty pressed into panic. In business the spark could be a customer's pain, a rival's insult, a market's blind spot.

- **Action.** Once lit, anger demands movement. Spears fly, code ships, campaigns launch, nights stretch. Raw drive turns plan into velocity.

- **Consequence.** Every action dents the world: Patroclus dies, Scamander floods, your servers buckle, or your product goes viral. Feedback lands—some of it scalding.

- **Meaning.** Humans stare at the dent and ask, *What now?* Achilles discovers compassion. Priam rediscovers courage. Start-up leaders absorb metrics, testimonies, fallout, and draft fresh purpose. Then new tensions arise and the loop recycles, spiraling upward if wisdom compounds or downward if hubris congeals.

The power of Homer's loop is that it offers no static victory. "Even the gods can be moved," Zeus muses, acknowledging perpetual unrest. Your company, your career, your life are likewise flux. The moment you pronounce "Done," unseen currents pool beneath. Better to treat every triumph as staging ground for the next iteration of the loop—anger tempered into vision, action refined by craft, consequence studied without vanity, meaning recast into bolder narrative.

---

2. Your One-Sentence Epic: A Challenge

Homer spends 15,693 lines charting the Iliad's arc, but the seed is that opening line. **You** now draft a single sentence to seed your own epic. It should do four things:

1. **Name the driving emotion.** "Frustration," "wonder," "defiance," "awe."

2. **Name the protagonist.** That may be you, your team, or the people you serve.

3. **Hint at the battlefield.** A domain, an industry, a social ill.

4. **Foreshadow transformation.** What meaning you hope the struggle will reveal.

Write it rough, then pare every extra syllable. Achilles' wrath sentence is ten heartbeats. Strive for similar rhythm.

Example drafts
 – "We ignite curiosity in classrooms that forgot how to ask why."
 – "I stand angry at wasted energy, and I will bend electrons toward justice."
 – "Together we mend digital trust where commerce broke it, so strangers can trade like friends."

Speak your sentence aloud until it stirs skin. Pin it above your screen. When anger flickers or consequence stings, recite it; meaning will surface, guiding the next swing of action.

---

3. Stewardship of Your Story

Remember, Homer never appears in his saga, yet his voice conditions every heartbeat. As leader, you are both character and poet. Your choices shape plot, but your storytelling—how you frame pivots, celebrate allies, mourn losses—determines whether talent stays invested. "'Let us record these deeds,'" cries the herald at Achilles' games; without record, greatness fades like camp-fire smoke.

Document. Keep battle logs, retros, demo videos.
 Mythologize. Turn launch failures into teaching parables.

Share authorship. Invite interns, users, even critics to annotate chapters. Their marginalia enrich the text and tame ego.

---

4. Ending Without Ending

The Iliad closes—Hector buried, dawn soft over Troy—yet we sense arrows nocked beyond sunrise. So will your venture end one day: exit, wind-down, reinvention. The goal is not to freeze success but to exit with doors open for new storytellers. "And so they buried Hector, tamer of horses," the last line says, and we inhale, eager for the Odyssey. Design your finale to spur sequels by alumni, acquirers, communities.

---

5. Step into the Sand

Lift pen or keyboard now. Draft that one sentence. Let it crackle. Then walk out your office door—literal or virtual—like Achilles in fresh armour, aware that rivers may rise, allies may falter, but meaning rides inside every stride if you keep the loop alive.

May the Muses track your metrics, may each setback forge deeper purpose, and may your own Iliad sing long after campfires dim.

THIS IS NOT A COLLECTION

This volume is part of **Ancient Wisdom Hacks**—
an ongoing body of work focused on how strategy, power, and
failure actually function under pressure.

The books are only one layer.

What you are reading is an entry point into a larger system of
interpretation, application, and expansion.

WHAT THESE WORKS ARE DESIGNED TO DO

Most people look for answers.

These works expose patterns:

- How decisions are made before they are visible
- How systems weaken before they collapse
- How power shifts before it is recognized

This is not theory.
It is applied observation.

THE SYSTEM BEHIND THE WORK

Across all volumes and future releases, three forces remain
constant:

- **Strategy** — how outcomes are shaped before action
- **Conflict** — how people and systems break under pressure
- **Power** — how control is gained, maintained, and lost

No single book contains the full picture.
Each adds another angle.

CONTINUE BEYOND THIS VOLUME

New interpretations, applied volumes, and extended works are released continuously.

To access current and future material, visit:

www.AncientWisdomHacks.com

WHAT YOU WILL FIND

- Additional applied volumes across industries
- Expanded interpretations of foundational texts
- New releases not available through standard distribution
- Future projects extending beyond books

The system is still expanding.

FINAL POSITION

Clarity does not make outcomes easier.

It removes the illusion that they were ever simple.

Ancient Wisdom Hacks
Interpretation over repetition.
Application over theory.